RUDOLF STEINER (1861–1925) called his spiritual philosophy 'anthroposophy', meaning 'wisdom of the human being'. As a highly developed seer, he based his work on direct knowledge and perception of spiritual dimensions. He initiated a modern and universal 'science of spirit', accessible to anyone willing to exercise clear and unprejudiced thinking.

From his spiritual investigations Steiner provided suggestions for the renewal of many activities, including education (both general and special), agriculture, medicine, economics, architecture, science, philosophy, religion and the arts. Today there are thousands of schools, clinics, farms and other organizations involved in practical work based on his principles. His many published works feature his research into the spiritual nature of the human being, the evolution of the world and humanity, and methods of personal development. Steiner wrote some 30 books and delivered over 6,000 lectures across Europe. In 1924 he founded the General Anthroposophical Society, which today has branches throughout the world.

Angels

Selected lectures by
Rudolf Steiner

Translated by Anna Meuss

RUDOLF STEINER PRESS

Compiled and edited by Wolf-Ulrich Klünker

Rudolf Steiner Press
Hillside House, The Square
Forest Row, East Sussex
RH18 5ES

www.rudolfsteinerpress.com

Published by Rudolf Steiner Press 1996
Reprinted 1998, 2001, 2007

Originally published in German under the title *Vom Wirken der Engel und anderer hierarchischer Wesenheiten* by Verlag Freies Geistesleben, Stuttgart, in 1991

A catalogue record for this book is available from the British Library

ISBN 978 185584 060 7

Cover by Andrew Morgan
Typeset by DP Photosetting, Aylesbury, Bucks.
Printed and bound in Great Britain by Cromwell Press Limited, Trowbridge, Wilts.

Contents

Introduction

by Wolf-Ulrich Klünker

In *Divisiones Naturae* (categories of nature), the chief work of the ninth-century Irish philosopher Johannes Scotus Erigena, we find the interesting statement: 'It is not without reason that we may believe and recognise that the incarnation of the Word of God is of as much service to the Angels as it is to man. To man it brought salvation and self-regeneration, to the Angels understanding and knowledge'.[1] The 'incarnation of the Word of God'—that is to say, Christ becoming man—has significance for both human beings and Angels. Erigena took this as self-evident. Our modern age, in contrast, sees Christ only in reference to humanity. In the ninth century it was obviously possible for people to understand the connection between themselves and the Angels in a quite different way. In the passage quoted above it is clear that Christ brought salvation to a fallen humanity, which, as a result, regained the possibility of freedom. The Angels, on the other hand, were neither redeemed nor restored to their original nature, but gained a different and higher form of knowledge.

The connection between the Angels and ourselves
What, then, is the difference which Erigena points to, between the Angels and ourselves? It is immediately clear that Angels have knowledge and understanding whereas we are in need of salvation and regeneration. The event which leads to our redemption serves to broaden and enrich the understanding and knowledge of Angels. We are not redeemed and regenerated only in the realm of our understanding and spiritual nature, but also in our bodies and souls. Christ's incarnation renews us in body, soul and spirit and we are able to recover

from sickness, from entanglements at soul level and lack of perception. Only the latter applies in the case of the Angels. In the angelic world—and this is the first, salient, feature of the relationship between the Angels and ourselves—changes that may take shape at the physical or soul level in humans appear only at the level of perception, of the spirit. To gain access to angelic regions we need to learn to transpose human experience into spiritual phenomena. The realm of spirit is the only reality known to Angels. In this respect we are different from, yet also united with, Angels: we are different because we do not dwell solely in a realm of knowledge and understanding, but we are the same in so far as *everything* we experience in body and soul can become spiritual reality in angelic regions.

Johannes Scotus Erigena refers to this in the following passage: 'God lives only within human and angelic nature, through which alone a perception of truth may be vouchsafed. We should not consider these two natures to be like two houses, but like a single house built of two spiritual materials.'[2] 'Nature' in this context signifies 'essence'. The difference between the two is made clear; yet it is also apparent that they are related to each other; they are 'neighbours'. They live in 'a single house', so that they meet all the time. Their proximity lies in the fact that they both perceive truth and can therefore gain knowledge and understanding. Nevertheless they are not identical in nature; Erigena describes them as 'two spiritual (*intelligibiles*) materials'. The human being has capacities of mental and spiritual perception like the Angel. But these appear in another form in him since he also has a body and a soul.

Some 250 years after Erigena, Alanus ab Insulis, a teacher in the School of Chartres in the twelfth century, described the difference between Angels and human beings in more detail. In *Quoniam Homines* he showed that we are not, by nature, equal to Angels in our understanding and perception, but can become so: 'Tradition has it that in time to come belief will be superseded by knowledge, by certain perception. Understanding will no longer be obscure and indistinct as it is in our times.' He then clarified what he meant by 'knowledge' (*scientia*): 'Knowledge is perception of the truth of things with inner accord, recognising their origins and causes.'[3] The indication is that human faculties of perception will change and that belief will be superseded by knowledge—an unheard-of assertion that was no doubt deeply shocking to the late twelfth-century attitude of mind, founded as it was so thoroughly on belief. For Alanus, this new faculty of perception would be 'certain' and therefore 'science', a term to be taken in a wider sense than we usually do today. It would be marked by 'inner accord' with what is perceived and by insight into its 'origins and causes'. This goes back to Aristotle. The human being would inwardly unite himself with the object of his perception, grasping it not only as it presents itself, but also in its origin and evolution. Alanus implies quite clearly that *we shall be equal to the Angels* when we achieve this mode of perception, suggesting a connection between the evolution of our faculties and our relationship to the higher hierarchies.

Knowing the Angels

Two generations later Thomas Aquinas (1225–74) made reference to the Gospel of Matthew (22, 30) with the words: 'To man is promised nothing less than equality with the Angels.'[4] Thomas thus also looked forward to a future stage of human evolution when we will have attained both the *understanding* and the *mode of existence* of Angels. He continued: 'The philosophers have taught that man's greatest happiness consists in thinking the beings that are separated from matter.'[5] 'Beings separated from matter' (*substantiae separatae a materia*) was the term used in philosophy for Angels, since they have no direct connection with the material world.

The importance of this statement becomes clear when we consider a further passage from the same text: 'In the realms which are separated from matter, the one who thinks is not different from what is thought.'[6] Thomas here refers to a statement in Aristotle's *De Anima* (book of the soul). The 'realms which are separated from matter' are angelic realms of existence, in which the process of perception and the object of perception cannot be distinguished: there is no separation between thinking subject and the object thought. Referring this passage back to the statement about 'man's greatest happiness', which consists in perceiving and thinking of angelic realms, we arrive at the following: when we attain knowledge and understanding of these realms, we enter a domain in which we become one with the object of perception. Knowledge of the Angels leads us therefore to being Angel-like ourselves. Knowledge and mode of existence here become one. To put it another way: when we develop to the point where we perceive in thought the essential nature of Angels, they are no longer an 'outer' object of understanding—we are transformed to be like unto the Angels. We become one with the Angels to the degree in which we learn to perceive and know them. This is, of course, only true in respect of our perceptive, spiritual existence; in our body and soul existence we remain different from the Angels, who are unembodied.

How can we attain angelic perception? In his *Summa Theologiae*, Thomas Aquinas offers three possible answers to this question, based on three different approaches in the history of philosophy. First he describes the position of Platonism: 'Plato holds that non-material beings are not only perceived and recognised by us, but that they also are what we first encounter. He asserts that the non-material, self-perpetuating forms which he names "ideas" are the true constituents of our spirit: it is for this reason that they are the first to be perceived by us, through their own original existence. According to him the soul directs its perception towards material things because the spirit is interfused with mental concepts and sensory perception. Therefore the more the spirit is purified, the more it will grasp the non-material, spiritual world.'[7]

This is how Thomas Aquinas characterizes the Platonic view at the point of contact between human and Angel spirit. He points out that Plato sees the 'non-material beings'—in other words, the Angels—as the original and ultimate object of human knowledge. But since the human spirit is not pure, mingled as it is with sensory perception and earthly concepts, we cannot perceive higher beings as a matter of course. When the mind and spirit frees itself from such earth-bound concerns, however, it may perceive these beings with the greatest clarity. It is clear that Plato hardly makes any distinction between human spirit and Angel. If we succeed in freeing ourselves from earthly perceptions and mental concepts, we can, in this view, perceive the angelic spirit as being of the *same nature* as ourselves, recognising in it our own ideal form of existence.

Thomas then wrote of the position taken by Aristotle: 'But according to Aristotle, who better substantiates our own experience, the human mind and spirit has a natural inclination towards the essence of material things. It therefore perceives nothing without having mental concepts about it. Thus it is clear that we cannot gain knowledge of non-material beings—who do not come under sensory perception and mental concepts—by the mode of knowledge which is innate in us.'[8] Thomas's summary of the Aristotelian position is therefore as follows: under earthly circumstances and conditions we can only gain knowledge through sensory perceptions of worldly things and from this develop mental concepts, for example as memories. We then reflect on such sensory impressions and concepts, deriving our knowledge from them. In earthly existence we have, in this view, a certain kind of knowledge which cannot serve us in the perception of higher beings; for these do not inhabit the world perceptible to the senses, nor are they accessible to our concepts. It is apparent that Thomas inclined more to the Aristotelian position. He believed the human spirit to be differently structured from the Angel spirit and therefore having separate and independent existence in regard to it. This means, however, that initially Angels are beyond the reach of human perception.

Finally, Thomas Aquinas sets beside these views the tenets of the twelfth-century Arab philosopher Averroës, commentator on Aristotle, who was a very significant figure in the Christendom of the Middle Ages. The position taken by Averroës could be seen as a third possibility for viewing the relationship between human spirit and Angel, and was indeed adopted by many thinkers of the time. Yet to Thomas it seemed dangerous: 'Averroës has asserted that it is possible, in this life, to perceive the beings separated from matter if one such being connects or becomes united with us; he terms such a being an "active spirit". Being a spiritual being the "active spirit" can of course perceive other spiritual beings. When it unites fully with us, so that we perceive fully through it, we can also perceive the beings separated from matter.'[9] The implications of this position are as follows: we do not attain to individual spiritual existence by means of such development, but partake of a cosmic angelic spirit. Such an angelic spirit is naturally in a position to recognise other angelic spirits. In this view we do not perceive the Angels in our capacity as human spirits, but by *becoming Angels in spirit*. We would then only perceive higher beings by forfeiting our individual human spirit. The position of Averroës is noticeably similar to that of Plato, though it originates in Aristotle.

Spiritual self-knowledge and knowledge of the Angels
Thomas Aquinas refuted the views of Averroës at great length. He believed that we should perceive the Angels by means of *applied thinking*, rather than through some convergence with a cosmic Angel spirit which 'has been conjectured by some people'. Thomas spoke of developing a perception of spiritual beings through the 'speculative sci-

ences'; these may lead to recognition of higher spirits by way
of *self-knowledge*. Building on the views of Aristotle, he came
to the conclusion that the study and knowledge of the human
soul was a sure foundation for perceiving higher spirits. 'For
by gaining knowledge of itself, our soul also attains knowledge, to some degree, of the unembodied spirits, in so far as
this is possible: it does not perceive them directly and completely, but only through its own self-perception.'[10]

The human spirit is not, according to this view, identical
with the Angels; it is, rather, human and individual. That is
why we cannot 'perceive them directly and completely'. The
human soul can draw near to the Angels by gaining spiritual
self-knowledge. One could add that the human spirit resides
within the human soul and is therefore differently constituted
from the Angel spirit which does not inhabit either a soul or
body. The spirit can only become individualised through
uniting with a body and soul.

According to Thomas, we should develop individuality of
spirit; for him, this was quite different from overcoming earthly
conditions and uniting with the angelic spirit. He believed that
the right way forward for perceiving higher beings was to
develop a 'science of the soul', by means of which we can know
ourselves spiritually. He saw this standpoint of the individuality of the human spirit as being in the Aristotelian tradition. He was opposed to the views of Averroës because they
related perception of Angels to cosmic rather than individual
human spirituality. Again drawing on Aristotle, he spoke of a
way of knowledge composed of two elements: the human
spirit's self-knowledge within the soul, and, founded upon it,
the perception of higher spiritual beings.

Such a conception was ahead of its time. In the Middle
Ages only the first hints existed of any attempt to develop a
'science of the soul' and approach the higher hierarchies
through active thinking. It was not until the advent of
anthroposophical spiritual science that this could be
continued and expanded. Rudolf Steiner's accounts of the

higher hierarchies invariably presuppose the spiritual individuality of human beings—without, however, losing sight of
the fact that we are not yet spiritually individual, but can
become so through self-development. As such, the views of
Rudolf Steiner on the Angel hierarchies follow on from
Aristotle and Thomas Aquinas. Yet there is no directly continued, philologically proven tradition at work here; it is rather
a spiritual inheritance which has resurfaced in quite new and
different historical circumstances.

The human being is capable of emancipating himself from
the sphere of cosmic spirituality; he can become independent
in spirit. However, by so doing he risks losing his awareness of
spiritual reality. This is, in actual fact, what has happened;
through our emancipation and development towards independence we have grown distant from the higher hierarchies.
We cannot usefully bridge this separation by attempting to re-
establish old forms of relationship, which would endanger our
spiritual independence. It was Rudolf Steiner's concern to
show ways in which we can know ourselves spiritually and so
develop spiritual individuality, thus establishing a quite new
relationship to the angelic sphere of reality.

New ways of approaching the Angels

Traditions of belief or theology cannot help us if we are to
attain knowledge of the reality of higher beings through
spiritual self-development and independence. Adherence to
any such tradition would hinder our spiritual freedom, as
would any categorized teaching or doctrine about the higher
hierarchies. Although Rudolf Steiner occasionally made
reference to the fifth-century teachings of Dionysius the
Areopagite on the hierarchies, he never made them the basis
of his descriptions. He would sometimes use the same terms
as Dionysius for distinguishing different realms of higher
beings—three hierarchies, each consisting of three orders—
but his approach was very different and he did not generally
use the Dionysian terminology.

Rudolf Steiner's descriptions do not form a doctrine; this would be antagonistic to a new knowledge of the Angels based on our spiritual individuality. They illumine a path rather than asserting a truth. It is apparent, however, that our ordinary thinking is not capable of attaining angelic reality; it needs to be transformed in order to do so. This is possible when it is activated in spiritual self-knowledge. Such self-knowledge is different and individual in each and every person; and the thinking which serves it remains individual when it reaches out to attain knowledge of other spiritual beings. This is the reason why doctrines of the higher hierarchies no longer have any place. The individuality of self-knowledge must pass over into this thought-illumined realm of spiritual reality. Thomas Aquinas' description of the unity of thinking and object in the realm of the higher hierarchies can be understood in the same way.

A second foundation and safeguard for the independence of human knowledge in the realm of higher hierarchies is that *thinking which attains to the sphere of the Angels must always be self-aware.* It cannot give its full attention only to the realm or object of its focus but must also retain conscious awareness of its own activity. Activity and object of perception belong indivisibly together in the realm of higher beings. If our thinking is directed only to the object of knowledge we can achieve merely *an image* of the higher hierarchies rather than their full reality. If, however, we simultaneously consider and include in our perception the *activated power* of our thinking in each moment, the image can become reality. Finally, we also become aware of a significant characteristic of spiritual self-knowledge—the fact that it is in a continual process of development. We do not know ourselves spiritually as we *are*, but as we evolve. Thinking that enters the realm of the Angels perceives itself as being in continual evolution.

Until our present time the conscious human mind could not gain access to the higher hierarchies by means of thinking. It is really only since the advent of the modern age that we have gradually begun to develop spiritual independence. A necessary part of this development has been our loss of awareness of the higher beings. If this had not occurred we would not have been able to stand upon our own two feet in our perception and knowledge; we would have continued to experience ourselves as spiritually dependent on the Angels—as was the case in the early Middle Ages. The fact that it is, in our day, increasingly difficult to experience their reality can be seen as a necessary step on the path towards ultimately perceiving them in independence of spirit. Rudolf Steiner's perception of the hierarchies comes to us at a moment in the development of human thinking when it begins to be possible once more to gain access to the reality of the sphere of the Angels.

To sum up, we need to consider our own thinking in two ways when seeking knowledge of the angelic realm: our thinking must always be aware of itself; it must also be capable of grasping the significance of its own transformation throughout human spiritual evolution. A person who has become spiritually independent has a different relationship to the Angels than was possible in an older form of consciousness. At the same time the reality of the Angel realm has altered for human beings; for in the domain of higher beings, thinking and the object of thought cannot be separated from one another.

From finished creation to creative power
We have seen how the connection between humanity and the higher hierarchies has altered as the human mind and spirit evolved. Strictly speaking, we can no longer talk of a relationship between humanity and higher beings, but only of one formed between them and an individual person. The reality of the hierarchies is now, and will be in the future, founded on spiritual individuality. In regard to the Angel, the individual person, like the whole of humanity, is involved in continual evolution and development. Such evolution and movement

allows nothing to remain still or finished and is the distinct characteristic of spiritual reality. In this perspective everything is seen in a process of becoming rather than in a state of completion. We must see ourselves, too, as developing rather than finished spiritual beings; only then can we draw near to the higher hierarchies. The task of our new capacity for knowledge is to complete the transition from perceiving what has become, what is finished creation, to knowing the world as a process of becoming. Then we can also begin to perceive what is actively at work as the origin and source of both. Such a source could also be described as a power working invisibly behind the finished world.

Initially, our human consciousness is aware only of this finished world. Through our senses we perceive phenomena which appear definite and complete; both in the realms of nature and in our social conditions we encounter apparently immutable facts and circumstances. We observe things as they *are*, not as they may *become*. We even tend to observe ourselves and others as we are at present rather than looking for as yet undeveloped potential. However, we can only grow conscious of spiritual reality by shifting our perception from finished to developing creation. Spiritual self-knowledge becomes possible only when we become aware of our own spiritual evolution. Then we can free ourselves from a widespread and tenacious dependence on the past without rejecting it wholesale; our past can become the *foundation for what we may become in the future*. Much the same would apply to our relationship to other human beings and to the world of nature.

We then need to make the further transition from a perception of processes of becoming to perception of the power and forces which cause and are at work within them. This means that one becomes aware of a spiritual individuality in oneself, the source and power which brings about one's own spiritual development. Such a transition, accomplished through oneself as a spiritual being, opens doors for us to the realms of the higher hierarchies, which are at work within the world we inhabit.

These two forms of transition are not as easy to accomplish as one might imagine. We are all bound up with the finished world through the force of deep-seated habit. We invariably tend to perceive facts rather than processes This can have catastrophic results in our relationship to nature. A factual thinking which relates only to what is already present can only come into play when something has 'occurred'; it cannot appraise future potential. In the realm of interpersonal relationships, such thinking becomes increasingly problematic. If we take account only of another person or a group as they appear to us in the present, not as they might become, we very soon have to face a breakdown in social relations. This is most obvious in the field of education, although it holds good for all areas of life. Education that recognizes only a child's present attributes and not his or her capacity for future development is doomed to failure.

Through practice one can gradually learn to perceive the reality of processes of becoming. This provides the basis for ultimate recognition of the forces at work within them. I would like, in conclusion, to clarify this second transition by a further reference taken from the work of Thomas Aquinas, one which also sheds light on our relationship with the Angels. In his *Summation of Theology*, Thomas asks how we should imagine the Angels' relationship to space. One answer is: 'It has been said that the Angel can, in certain respects, be present at a physical location by directing its power towards it . . . a non-physical being which through its power has contact with a physical thing, holds it and is not held by it . . . therefore it is said that the Angel resides at a physical location as upholder, not as one upheld.'[12]

The Angel, then, is not present at a particular place in a spatial sense, but by directing its power towards this place. Its power 'holds' the things of that place; this does not mean 'holding fast to', but rather a spiritual configuring of the place with the help of the things present in it. The Angel 'holds' a particular place by using its power to configure and uphold it. In contrast, objects perceived by the senses are 'held' rather than 'holding'. They are dependent on location, which determines their appearance and constitution. One can observe this in the dependence of a plant on its habitat. The Angels, on the other hand, are not determined by, but determine the place of their activity. In contrast to all physical things, the Angel is 'not circumscribed (by space) ... but encompasses it.'[13] We can glean from this passage how we might pass from a defined and 'finished' perception of nature to an awareness of its 'becoming' and ultimately of the creative power at work within it.

The lectures selected for this volume

The three sections of this book deal with three spheres of activity of higher beings: human individuality, human evolution and cosmic reality. Some of the lecture titles were taken from the Complete Edition of the works of Rudolf Steiner, others were newly formulated. This selection cannot claim to represent all aspects of the higher hierarchies addressed by Rudolf Steiner; each section, nevertheless, tries to illuminate as broad a spectrum as possible within the given theme. Some lectures are taken from series of lectures whose overall content determines the particular perspective. In such a case, as also with individual lectures, it is the complete context and the whole view which is important, rather than isolated statements. The reader will therefore need to find his way to an understanding of the whole direction and context of each separate lecture. The lectures taken from a series were selected so as to allow such an understanding without presupposing familiarity with the whole series.

The practice of comprehending a complete context rather than isolated statements is an essential one: it is not an additional activity, separate from 'normal' reading, but fundamental to understanding. What is decisive in this process is the initial *intention* of keeping the context in mind; this enables one to have a different kind of understanding than is possible by simply connecting separate statements as one goes along. It is less important whether one gains an immediate insight into the context or not; this is likely only to be a question of time, as with all meditative practice. Many passages which might appear problematic in isolation can be understood within their context. Many apparent 'contradictions' between statements in different lectures, for example, will be resolved by reference to the varying perspectives they offer. The intricate realms of reality of the higher hierarchies cannot be illumined by individual definitive statements.

In fact, Rudolf Steiner's descriptions of higher beings can encourage us to extend our focused consciousness, enlarge it to a contextual understanding. The first step in this process would involve re-reading a lecture many times, allowing a gap between each reading during which one would recall its content in quiet contemplation. Then one could continue by building up an inner picture of the relationship between two lectures in the same section of this volume. Later on one might attempt to do this with all the lectures in one section. Having done this with the three separate sections of the book, one might finally relate these sections to each other. Anyone who would also like to occupy himself with the 'whole' context of Rudolf Steiner's observations on the hierarchies should refer especially to *Occult Science—an Outline*[14] and *Spiritual Guidance of the Individual and Humanity*.[15] The latter deals particularly with the theme of spiritual hierarchies and human individuality while the former is more concerned with the themes addressed in sections 2 and 3 of this volume—spiritual hierarchies in human evolution and spiritual hierarchies as cosmic reality.

I. SPIRITUAL HIERARCHIES AND HUMAN INDIVIDUALITY

1. The Work of the Angel in our Astral Body

Zurich, 9 October 1918

Anthroposophical understanding of the spirit must be a leaven, a real power in life, and not merely a theoretical view of life. It can really only fulfil its mission if we develop the inner powers that allow it to come fully alive in us. Connecting with the anthroposophical conception of the spirit we become custodians, as it were, of quite specific, significant processes in human evolution.

Whatever their view of the world, people are generally convinced that thoughts and ideas have no place in it, except as the contents of their own souls. People who hold such views believe that thoughts and ideas as ideals are only embodied in the world to the extent that a person succeeds in implementing them by his physical actions.

The anthroposophical approach asks us to accept that thoughts and ideas must also find other ways of coming to realization. Recognition of this essential principle implies that anthroposophists must play their part in watching out for the signs of the times. A great deal is happening all the time in world evolution; and it falls to human beings, particularly those of our own time, to acquire real understanding of the world events in which they are involved.

We know that with individual human beings account must be taken of their stage of development as well as external events around them. Just think, putting it very crudely, that events are now happening around individuals who are 5, 10, 20, 30, 50 or 70 years of age. No one in their senses would expect the same reaction from 5-, 10-, 20-, 50- and 70-year-olds. The way people may be expected to react to their environment can only be determined by taking account of their stage of development. Everyone will admit this to be true in the individual case.

Just as there are definite stages in individual development, with the nature of our powers and faculties different in childhood, mid-life and old age, so are the powers and faculties humanity has as a whole always changing in the course of evolution.

Failing to take note of the fact that the character of twentieth-century humanity differs from that of humanity in the fifteenth century, let alone before and at the time of the Mystery of Golgotha, is to sleep through the process of world evolution. One of the greatest defects, one of the principal sources of error and confusion in our time, is the failure to take note of this, thinking in terms of abstract generalization of individuals or of humanity, with no need to know that humanity is in a process of evolution.

The question is, how can we gain fuller insight into these things? As you know, we have often spoken of one important phase in human evolution. The Graeco-Latin period of civilisation, from the eighth century BC to approximately the fifteenth century, was the period when the intellectual or mind soul evolved. Development of the spiritual soul has been in progress from the fifteenth century, a factor in human evolution that concerns our own time in particular. We know that the paramount factor in human evolution from the fifteenth century to the beginning of the fourth millennium is the spiritual soul.

In a true science of the spirit we must never stop at generalizations and abstractions. Always and in all places we must endeavour to grasp the real situation. Abstractions will at most satisfy our curiosity in the ordinary sense of the word. To make the science of the spirit the leaven and essential power in our life we must be profoundly serious rather than curious, and not stop at such abstractions. It is both true and important that living in the age of the spiritual soul we must take special account of its development; but we must not stop there.

To gain a clear conception of these things we must above all consider the nature of man himself in greater detail. In terms of the science of the spirit, the aspects of the human being, from above down, are ego, astral body, ether body—which I have more recently also called the body of generative forces—and physical body. The ego is the only one of these in which we live and function in soul and spirit. It has been given to us through Earth evolution and the Spirits of Form who direct it. Essentially everything that enters into conscious awareness does so through the ego. If the ego did not evolve in a way that allows it to remain connected with the outside world—even just indirectly, through the astral, ether and physical bodies—we would have as little conscious awareness as we have during sleep. It is the ego which connects us with our environment; the astral body is the legacy of the Old Moon evolution that preceded Earth evolution, the ether body of Old Sun evolution, the physical body, in its first rudiments, of Old Saturn evolution.

If you study the description of these bodies in *Occult Science—An Outline*,[14] you will perceive the complex nature of the process in which this fourfold constitution of man came into being. The facts presented in the book clearly show that all the hierarchies were involved in the creation of the astral, etheric and physical bodies, and we can see that these enveloping forms are highly complex by nature. The hierarchies have not only been involved in their creation—they are still active in them. People who think the human being to be merely a combination of bones, blood, flesh, and so on, which is the view held in modern science, physiology, biology or anatomy, do not understand his true nature.

If we consider the reality of these aspects of the human being, perceiving the truth of them, we realize that spirits of the hierarchies are working together in everything that goes on in those bodies without our being conscious of it. From the brief outline of the concerted actions of individual spirits from the hierarchies I have given in *Occult Science—An Outline* you can see how intricate the details must be. Nevertheless, if we want to understand the human being we must go into this further.

It is extremely difficult to consider a specific issue in this field. The situation is highly complex. Suppose someone were to ask: What is the hierarchy of the Seraphim or of the Dynamis doing in the human ether body at the present time in human evolution, in the year 1918? We may ask this just as we may ask whether it happens to be raining in Lugano. Neither question can be answered by merely reflecting or theorizing on it, only by ascertaining the facts. We might send a telegram or a letter, for instance, to find out if it is raining in Lugano. And we must also enter into the facts of the situation if we want to know, say, what is the mission of the Spirits of Wisdom or of the Thrones as far as the human ether body is concerned at the present time. This, however, is an extremely complex issue, and we will never be able to do more than get a bit closer to the areas where such questions arise. Good care is taken that we shall not soar too far aloft and become arrogant and supercilious in our search for knowledge.

The spirits we can see most clearly may be said to be those nearest to us, the ones that directly concern us. And it is important that we see them clearly if we are not to remain asleep at our stations in human evolution.

I am therefore going to speak of something that is less vague and indefinite than the question as to what the Dynamis or Thrones are doing in the human etheric body. A question of immediate concern to people today is what the Angels, the spirits nearest to humanity, are doing in the human astral body at the present time.

The astral body is closest to the ego, so that finding an answer to this question would be of real concern to us. The Angels are the hierarchy immediately above the human hierarchy. We shall ask the modest question as to what the Angels are doing in the human astral body at the present time, a stage in the life of humanity that started in the fifteenth century and will continue to the beginning of the fourth millennium, and we shall find the answer to be really important to us.

What can actually be said when it comes to answering a question such as this? Only that spiritual investigation pursued in all seriousness is not a matter of juggling with ideas or words, but truly takes us into regions where the world of the spirit can be perceived, which is in the regions nearest to us. A truly useful answer can only be found now, in the age of the spiritual soul.

You might think that if this question could have been asked in other times an answer may well have been forthcoming. But it could not have been answered in the age of atavistic clairvoyance nor in the period of Graeco-Latin civilization because the images arising in the mind's eye from atavistic clairvoyance would have obscured anything perceived of the Angel's activities in the astral body. Nothing could be seen of them precisely because human beings had the images that came from atavistic clairvoyance. In Graeco-Latin times people did not have the thinking power they have today. Our thinking power has increased, especially with the evolution of modern science, and in the age of the spiritual soul such a question can be the subject of deliberate study. The fruits which the science of the spirit can have in life must be evident from the fact that we do not just dole out theories but know how to say things of incisive significance for life.

What are the Angels doing in our astral body? We can discover this if we progress to a level of clairvoyant observation that enables us to see what happens in the astral body. We have to achieve a certain level at least of perception in images if we are to answer the question.

We then find that the spirits from the hierarchy of the Angels—and in a way this means each individual Angel who has a mission relating to every individual human being and also their concerted actions—shape images in the human astral body under the guidance of the Spirits of Form. We have to reach the level of perception in images before we can

know that images are being shaped all the time in our astral
body. They arise and pass away, but without them mankind
would not evolve according to the intentions of the Spirits of
Form. Initially the Spirits of Form are obliged to develop
images of what they want to achieve with us during Earth
evolution. Later these images become reality in a humanity
transformed.

Today the Spirits of Form are creating images in us through
the Angels. These images can be perceived with thinking
developed to become clairvoyant. We then find that the
images are created according to quite definite impulses and
principles. Forces for the future evolution of humanity lie in
the way these images are created. If we watch the Angels at
their work—this may sound strange but that is how it has to be
put—we find they have a very definite plan for the future
configuration of social life on Earth; their aim is to create
images in human astral bodies that will bring about definite
conditions in the social life of the future.

People may shy away from the notion that Angels want to
call forth ideals for the future in them, but that is how it is.
The process follows a specific principle, which is that in time
to come no human being shall find peace in the enjoyment of
happiness if others around him are unhappy. An impulse of
absolute brotherliness, making all of humanity one, will
govern social life. This principle of brotherliness regarding
social conditions in physical life will have to be thoroughly
understood.

This is one principle according to which the Angels create
images in the human astral body.

There is also another impulse. They have specific objectives
not only with regard to outer social life but also for the inner
life. Here the aim they pursue with the images imprinted in
the astral body is that in future every human being shall see a
hidden divine principle in every other human being.

Mark you well, the intention underlying the work of the
Angels is that things shall change. In future we shall not

consider human beings to be higher animals, considering their physical qualities in both theory and practice. Instead we are to meet every other human being with the full realization that something of the divine foundations of the world is revealing itself in flesh and blood. To conceive man as an image revealed out of the world of the spirit, and do so in profound seriousness, with all our strength—that is the impulse the Angels lay into the images.

Once this is brought to realization there will be a definite consequence. All independent religious feeling developing in humanity in time to come will depend on the individual being recognized in the image of God in real, practical terms and not mere theory. There will then be no need for religious compulsion, for every encounter between individuals will be a religious act, a sacrament, and there will be no more need for a church with physical buildings and institutions to maintain religious life. The church, if it understands itself rightly, must consider it to be its sole aim to render itself superfluous on the physical plane as the whole of life becomes an expression of the realm that lies beyond the senses. Such, at least, is the reason behind the work of the Angels—to bestow complete religious freedom on humanity.

A third objective is to enable human beings to reach the spirit through thinking, crossing the abyss and experiencing the reality of the spirit in their thinking.

Science of the spirit for mind and spirit, religious freedom for the soul, brotherliness for our bodies—this is like cosmic music resounding through the work which the Angels do in the human astral body. All we have to do is raise our consciousness to a different level and we shall feel ourselves transported to this wonderful place of work which the Angels have in the human astral body.

We are in the age of the spiritual soul, when the Angels do the work I have just described in the human astral body. Humanity must gradually come to be fully conscious of this. It is part of human evolution.

How is it possible to say the kind of thing I have just been saying? Where are we to look for this work of the Angels? Today we still find it in human sleep states, including states of waking sleep. I have often said that even when they are awake people actually sleep through the most important concerns in life. And I can assure you, though you may not be pleased to hear it, that anyone who goes through life with a wide-awake mind will find numbers and numbers of people who are really asleep. They let events happen without taking the slightest interest in them, without troubling their heads over them or connecting with them in any way. Great world events often pass people by just as something happening in the city passes by someone who is asleep; yet those people are ostensibly awake. When people are thus sleeping through some momentous event it can be seen that the Angels are doing their important work in their astral bodies—quite independently of what these people do or do not want to know.

Such things often happen in a way which must necessarily seem highly enigmatic and distinctly odd. We may think some people completely unworthy of entering into any connection with the world of the spirit. But the truth may well be that in this incarnation the person is an absolute dormouse who sleeps through everything that goes on around him. And in his astral body a spirit from the community of Angels is working on the future of mankind. Observation of this astral body shows that it is being used in spite of those conditions.

What really matters, however, is that human beings grow conscious of these things. The spiritual soul must rise to the level where it is able to recognize what can only be discovered in this particular way.

You will now have sufficient background to understand me when I say that this age of the spiritual soul is moving towards a specific event. Because it involves the spiritual soul you will understand that the effect this event has on human evolution will depend on human beings themselves. This may be a century earlier or a century later, but it is bound to be part of the evolutionary process. It can be characterized by saying that purely out of the spiritual soul, purely out of conscious thinking, human beings must reach the point of actually perceiving what the Angels are doing to prepare the future of humanity. The things we learn through the science of the spirit must become practical wisdom in the life of humanity—so practical that people will be convinced it is part of their own wisdom to recognize the aims of the Angels as I have described them.

The progress of the human race towards freedom has already reached a point where it will depend on human beings themselves whether they are going to sleep through this event or face it in wide-awake consciousness. To meet it in full consciousness would mean this: We can study the science of the spirit. Indeed nothing else is really necessary. It also helps to meditate and use the guidance given in *Knowledge of the Higher Worlds.*[16] But the essential step has already been taken if the science of the spirit has been studied and really consciously understood. Today it can be studied without developing clairvoyant faculties.

Everyone can do so who does not bar his own way with his prejudices. And if people study the science of the spirit more and more thoroughly, assimilating its concepts and ideas, their conscious mind will become so alert that they will be fully aware of events and no longer sleep through them.

We can characterize these events in greater detail. Essentially knowing what the Angel is doing is only a preparation. The important point is that three things will happen at a particular point in time. As I said, depending on how people respond, the time may be earlier or later, or, at worst, they may not happen at all. But the intention is that humanity shall be shown three things by the angelic world.

Firstly, it will be shown that their own genuine interest will enable people to understand the deeper side of human nature. A time will come—and it must not pass unnoticed—when human beings will receive an impulse from the world of the spirit through the Angel. This will kindle a far deeper interest in every human individual than we are inclined to have today. Enhanced interest in other human beings will not be of the subjective kind we like to develop at our leisure, but there will be a sudden impetus and a secret will be instilled into us from the realm of the spirit, the secret of what the other person really is. This is something quite real and specific, not any kind of theoretical consideration. People will learn something and this will kindle their interest in every human being. This is the one event, and it will particularly affect the social sphere.

The second event will be that the Angel irrefutably shows the human being that apart from all else the Christ impulse means complete religious freedom for humanity and that the only true Christianity is one that makes absolute religious freedom possible.

The third event will be that we gain irrefutable insight into the spiritual nature of the world.

As I have said, the three events should take place in such a way that the spiritual soul in us participates in it. This is something that will happen in human evolution, with the Angels now working to this end through the images they create in the human astral body.

Let it be emphasized, however, that this impending triple event is subject to man's free will. Many things that should lead to conscious awareness of the event may be and indeed are being left undone.

As you know, other spirits involved in world evolution have an interest in deflecting mankind from its proper course. These are the ahrimanic and luciferic spirits. The events I have just described are part of the divine evolution of man. If people were to follow the dictates of their own true nature they could not really fail to perceive what the Angels are doing in their astral body. But luciferic spirits seek to divert human beings concerning insight into the work of the Angels. They do this by curbing free will. They try to cloud our understanding of the exercise of our free will. True, they desire to make us good—from the point of view from which I am now speaking Lucifer desires goodness, spirituality, for mankind—but he wants to make us into automatons, with no free will. Human beings are to be made clairvoyant according to perfectly good principles, but in an automatic way; the luciferic spirits want to deprive human beings of their free will, the possibility of doing evil.

This has to do with specific secrets of evolution. As you know, the luciferic spirits have remained stationary at other levels of evolution and bring something foreign into the normal evolutionary process. They are deeply interested in seizing hold of us and preventing us from gaining free will because they themselves have not achieved it. Free will can be gained only on Earth, but the luciferic spirits want to have nothing to do with the Earth; they want only old Saturn, Old Sun and Old Moon evolution and nothing beyond this. In a sense they hate human free will. They act in a highly spiritual but automatic way—this is highly significant—and want to raise human beings to their own spiritual heights, making them spiritual but automatic. On the one hand this would create the danger that, before the spiritual soul is fully functional, human beings become spiritual automatons and sleep through the revelation that is to come, which I have characterised for you.

Ahrimanic spirits are also working against this revelation. They do not seek to make human beings particularly spiritual but to smother their awareness of their own spirituality. They want to teach people that they are really only a perfectly developed animal. Ahriman is in truth the great teacher of materialistic Darwinism. He also teaches all the technological and practical activity in Earth evolution where nothing is considered valid unless it can be perceived by the senses, the desire being to have widespread technology, with people satisfying their needs for food and drink and other things in the same way as animals do, except that it is more sophisticated. To kill and obscure man's awareness that he is an image of the godhead—this is the aim ahrimanic spirits are seeking to achieve by sophisticated scientific means in our age.

In earlier times it would have been of no avail for the ahrimanic spirits to obscure the truth for human beings by means of theories. The reason was that in Graeco-Latin times, and even more so before then, people still gained images through atavistic clairvoyance and it did not matter what they thought. They had their images which were like windows into the world of the spirit. Anything Ahriman might have taught them concerning their relation to animals would have had no effect on their way of life. Thinking only became a powerful process—powerful in its impotence, we might say— in our fifth post-Atlantean age, from the fifteenth century onwards. Only then did thinking become effective in taking the spiritual soul into the realm of the spirit or, indeed, preventing it from entering into the world of the spirit. Only now do we live in an age when a scientific theory may be deliberately used to deprive us of our divine nature and all experience of divine nature. This is only possible in the age of the spiritual soul. The ahrimanic spirits therefore seek to spread teachings among humanity that obscure man's divine origin.

This reference to the streams that go against normal and divine human evolution may show how we must conduct our lives so that we do not sleep through the revelation that is to come. Otherwise a great danger will arise. We have to be on the alert for this, or something will develop that may be a great and real danger to Earth evolution, taking the place of the significant event intended to play a momentous part in shaping the future evolution of Earth.

Some spiritual beings achieve higher development because human beings develop together with them. The Angels do not develop images in the human astral body as a kind of game but in order to achieve something. As the aim they have to achieve lies within earthly humanity itself, the whole matter would become a game if human beings, having reached the stage of the spiritual soul, were to deliberately ignore it. This would make it all into a game. The Angels would be playing a game in the developing human astral body. It is not a game but a serious business only because it comes to realization in humanity. You will realize, therefore, that the work of the Angels must always be a serious matter. Imagine what would happen behind the scenes of existence if human beings were to stay asleep and so turn the work of the Angels into a game!

What if this were to happen after all? What if earthly humanity were to persist in sleeping through the momentous spiritual revelation that is to come? If humanity were to sleep through the middle part, for instance, the matter relating to religious freedom, if they were to sleep through the repetition of the Mystery of Golgotha on the etheric plane, the reappearance of the etheric Christ, or through other things, the Angels would have to achieve their aim in a different way. If human beings did not, while awake, allow the Angels to achieve their aim in human astral bodies, they would achieve it with the help of the physical and ether bodies that remain in bed during sleep. This is where powers to achieve the aim would be sought. The aim not achievable with human beings who are awake, with souls awake in their ether and physical bodies, will be achieved with the ether and physical bodies as they lie asleep, when human beings who should be awake are outside those bodies with their ego and astral body.

Here lies the great danger for the age of the spiritual soul. It may still happen if human beings are not willing to turn to life in the spirit before the beginning of the third millennium. The third millennium begins in the year 2000, and is therefore only a short way ahead of us. It may still be necessary for the Angels to achieve their aim by means of sleeping human bodies. They would have to withdraw all their work from the astral body and take it into the etheric body to do so. But then the human being would have no part in it. The work would have to be done in the ether body when the human being is not present, for if he were present in the waking state he would obstruct it.

This gives you a general idea. But what would be the out-come if the Angels were obliged to do their work without the participation of human beings, doing it in human ether and physical bodies during sleep?

The inevitable effect on human evolution would be three-fold. Firstly, something would be engendered in sleeping human bodies, when the human ego and astral body are outside, which human beings would not discover in freedom but simply find to be there when they wake up in the morning. Danger would threaten from certain instinctive perceptions connected with the mystery of birth and conception and with sexual life as a whole that are intended to be part of human nature. The danger would come from certain Angels who themselves would undergo a change, which is something I cannot speak about, for it belongs to the higher secrets of initiation which may not yet be disclosed. But this much can certainly be said: The effect on human evolution would be that certain instincts belonging to the sexual life and to sexual nature would not come to clear conscious awareness in a useful way but become harmful. These instincts would not be mere aberrations but would enter into the social life, config-uring it. Something would enter into people's blood as a consequence of sexual life that would above all make people go against brotherliness on Earth rather than develop broth-erliness. This would be a matter of instinct.

A crucial time will come when the path to the right may be taken—which demands wakefulness—or the path to the left, where people sleep. Instincts of a truly horrific nature would then develop.

What do you suppose scientific experts will say when such instincts emerge? They will consider them a natural and inevitable development in human evolution. Light cannot be shed on such matters by ordinary science, for scientific rea-soning can be used to explain why people become angels or devils. In either case one thing always follows from another—the great wisdom of causality! Scientists will be completely blind to the event of which I have spoken, for they will simply consider it to be a natural necessity that people turn into half devils because of their sexual instincts. There can be no scientific explanation, for anything and everything can always be explained in science. The fact is that such things can only be understood by spiritual insight that goes beyond the sphere of the senses.

Secondly, this work, which also brings changes for the Angels, will cause humanity to gain instinctive knowledge of some medicines, and harmful knowledge of others. Everything connected with medicine will make great advances in the materialistic sense. People will gain instinctive insight into the medicinal properties of some substances and techniques and this will cause tremendous damage but would be said to be beneficial. Pathological changes will be called normal, for people will find that this leads to a certain technique that pleases them. They will actually like things that in a certain way take humanity into an unhealthy state. Knowledge of the medicinal powers of certain processes and techniques will increase but this will lead into very harmful channels. Out of certain instincts people will know the kind of diseases which can be produced by specific substances and techniques, and they will be able to arrange matters entirely to suit their egotistical purposes, to provoke diseases or not to provoke them.

Thirdly, humanity will get to know specific powers which enable them to unleash tremendous mechanical forces in the world by means of quite simple manipulations—bringing certain wave-lengths into accord. They will instinctively come to realize that it is possible to exercise some degree of mental control over mechanics. This will take the whole of technology along disastrous channels, a state of affairs, however, that will serve human egotism extremely well and please people.

Here we gain clear insight into the evolution of existence, and we perceive a conception of life that can really only be properly appreciated by those who understand that we shall never be clear about these things if we take an unspiritual view of life. People with an unspiritual view of life would not be able to perceive that an approach to medicine was causing harm to humanity, that sexual instincts were going desperately astray, that a terrible hustle and bustle of purely mechanistic activity was arising as forces of nature were utilized through powers of the mind. They would not realize that this meant deviation from the true path, just as someone who is asleep cannot see the thief who comes to rob him; the incident would pass him by; at most he would realize what had happened later, after he had woken up. But it would be a terrible awakening for humanity. People would delight in the instinctive broadening of their knowledge of certain processes and substances; they would gain a certain satisfaction in the pursuit of sexual aberrations, regarding them as evidence of an advanced development of more than human qualities, lack of prejudice and broad-mindedness. In some respects ugliness would be considered beauty and beauty ugliness. None of this would be noticed for it would be taken for natural necessity. It would, however, be a deviation from the path laid down for humanity in the individual nature given to human beings.

I think if we develop a feeling for the way the science of the spirit enters into our attitudes of mind we can also be truly serious in our approach to truths like those presented today, and gain from them what really should be gained from the whole of this science: to recognize a certain obligation, certain responsibilities in life. Whatever our role in life and in the world, it is important that we have the thought: Everything we do must be imbued with and illumined by anthroposophical awareness. We then contribute something to the true advancement of human evolution.

It would be entirely wrong to believe that the true science of the spirit, approached in a serious and worthy mood, could ever divert us from the necessary practical involvement in life. The true science of the spirit makes us wake up with regard to such matters as I have spoken of today.

You may, of course, ask if waking life is harmful to sleep. If we take the analogy that insight into the world of the spirit means to waken at a higher level than we do when we wake from sleep, we may also ask the question, in order to understand the analogy: Can this kind of waking life ever be harmful to sleep? Yes, if it is not what it ought to be! If people spend their waking life as it should be spent, they will also sleep soundly; if they doze through their waking hours, or are lazy, taking the easy way, their sleep will not be sound. The same holds true for the waking life we acquire by working with the science of the spirit. If the science of the spirit helps us to establish a proper relationship to the world of the spirit, this will also guide our interest in the familiar, sense-perceptible aspects of life along the right channels, just as a proper waking life gives sound sleep.

Looking at life in our time we must indeed be asleep if we fail to notice a number of things. Think how people have preened themselves on their conduct of life, particularly in the last few decades! They have finally reached a point where leading positions are held everywhere by people who are utterly contemptuous of the life of ideas, of the spirit. People have gone on to hold forth about their life style, for so far humanity has not been dragged into the abyss. Now, however, some begin to croak, albeit most of them instinctively: A new age must come, all kinds of new ideals must arise! But they are croaking. If these things were to come instinctively, without consciously making the science of the spirit one's own, they would lead to a decline of what should be experienced in the waking state and not to any kind of wholesome transition in evolution.

Anyone who today makes impassioned speeches to people in words they have long been accustomed to hear can usually still count on some applause. But people will have to get used to listening to different words, different ways of putting things, if a social cosmos is to arise from the chaos.

If human beings fail to wake up in a particular era and fail to discover what needs to be done, nothing real will happen. Instead, the spectre of the preceding era will arise. Thus spectres of the past are to be found in many religious communities today, and the spectre of ancient Rome still haunts the sphere of jurisprudence. The science of the spirit exists to make people free in this respect in the age of the spiritual soul, truly guiding them to observe a spiritual fact: What is the work of the Angels in our astral bodies? To talk about Angels and so on in an abstract way can at most be a beginning. Progress requires that we speak in real terms, that is, find the answer to the most immediate question in our present age. This concerns us because the Angel is creating images in our astral body, images that are to configure us for the future, a configuration to be achieved by the spiritual soul.

Without a spiritual soul there would be no need to exert ourselves. Other spirits, other hierarchies would step in and bring the images created by the Angels to fulfilment. We are, however, intended to develop a spiritual soul, and because of this no other spirits come to bring the work of the Angels to fruition.

Angels were, of course, also at work in the Egyptian era. But other spirits soon came in, and as a result man's atavistic clairvoyance became obscured. Seeing this in their atavistic clairvoyance, human beings wove a dark veil to cover the work of the Angels. Now, however, human beings must remove the veil. They should not sleep through what is being brought into conscious life in an age that will reach its conclusion before the third millennium. Let us draw not only teachings but also resolves from the science of the spirit extended by anthroposophy! Such resolves will give us the strength to be vigilant and alert.[17]

We can get into the habit of being alert. We can pay heed to many things. We can make a start now and find that basically not a day passes without a miracle happening in our life. We can also put this the other way round and say: If we do not discover a miracle in our life on a particular day, we have merely lost sight of it. Try to look back on your life in the evening; you will find some event—small, middling or great—of which you will be able to say that it came into your life and took effect in a remarkable way. You can achieve this if you take a wide enough view, considering the circumstances and connections in life on a sufficiently wide scale. But we do not usually do this in ordinary life, because we do not normally ask ourselves what has been prevented from happening in some way, for example.

We do not usually trouble about things that have been prevented, though if they had happened they would have brought a fundamental change in our lives. Behind the things which have been kept out of our lives in some way or other lies a great deal of what makes us into alert human beings. What might have happened to me today? If I ask myself this question every night and then consider individual occurrences that might have had one consequence or another, reflections on life will arise in connection with these questions that bring the element of vigilance into my self-discipline. Thus a start can be made, and it will take us further and further, until finally we explore not only what it means in our life that we intended to go out at half past ten in the morning, for example, but someone turned up at the last minute and stopped us. It annoys us that we were stopped, but we do not ask what might have happened if we really had gone out at the intended time. We do not consider what change there has been.

I have spoken of these things in greater detail here on an earlier occasion. A straight and certain path leads from observation of negative aspects in our lives, which may bear witness to wise guidance, to observation of the Angel who is actively working in our astral body. It is a path that is open to us.

2. Three Encounters between the Human Soul and Spirits of the Universe

Berlin, 20 February 1917

If we are able to make real, practical use, in the best possible sense, of the insights to be gained from the science of the spirit, we may begin to realize that we have a second, inner, human being inside the ordinary human being we know, definitely a second human being. In this respect all of us really consist of two beings. One essentially consists of the physical and the etheric body, and is part of the outside world—outside world in the sense that the physical body, and in some respects also the etheric body, are product and image, revelation of the divine spirits that surround us. In their true nature, not the way we usually know them, our physical body and ether body are images not of ourselves, nor of our personal reality, but images of the gods, we might say, who come into their own in producing our physical body and ether body and causing the two to develop. The inner human being is more closely related to the astral body and the I, or ego. This I and the astral body are younger, in the eyes of the universe, than the physical and ether bodies. This has been discussed in *Occult Science—An Outline*.[14] The I and the astral body may be said to rest in a bed prepared for us by the divine spirits who are present throughout the universe, bringing it to revelation. Thanks to the events, trials, tribulations and destiny that the I and astral body go through within the physical and etheric bodies, they will gradually progress through the developmental stages we have been discussing.

We are closely bound up with the whole universe, the whole cosmos, as I said in my last lecture.[18] Our relationship to the cosmos can actually be put in figures; it can be calculated, as we have seen from the quick sum I did last time. It may also come to expression in many other ways, but the surprising fact is that it can be stated in figures, for instance that the number of breaths we take in a day is also the number of years the Sun needs to return to the same place in its orbit at the spring equinox. If we allow such a discovery to enter our feelings, we may know shivers of holy awe at the thought of being at one with the divine and spiritual universe as it comes to revelation in all things.

At a much deeper level this shows that we are the small world, the microcosm, that comes to revelation out of the great world, the macrocosm. To realize this we must consider such facts as I am going to present today, facts I would like to call the three encounters between the human soul and spirits of the universe.

We know that as human beings we have a physical body and an ether body, an astral body and our I. Each of the two human beings in us has two sub-aspects, we might say: the more external aspect of physical body and ether body and the more inward one of I and astral body. We also know that humanity will evolve further. The Earth as we know it will one day come to an end. It will continue to evolve through Jupiter, Venus and Vulcan stages. Humanity will progress from stage to stage. In addition to the I, a higher aspect will reveal itself in human beings: the Spirit Self. This will essentially develop during the Jupiter stage of evolution which will follow the Earth stage. The Life Spirit will come to full revelation during the Venus stage, and the true Spirit Man on Vulcan. Looking ahead to a great cosmic future, we thus see three stages: the evolution of Spirit Self, Life Spirit and Spirit Man. In a way, these three future developments have a connection with us even today, when they have not yet developed in us, for they have been decided upon and still lie in the lap of the divine spirits we know as the higher hierarchies. They are the gift given to us by those spirits and we are already in touch with these higher hierarchies who in time to come will give us Spirit

Self, Life Spirit and Spirit Man. Instead of making the complex statement: 'We are in touch with the hierarchy of the Angels', we may therefore say: 'We are in touch with the Spirit Self which will be ours in the future.' And instead of saying: 'We are in touch with the Archangels,' we say: 'We are in touch with the future Life Spirit', and so on.

And it is true that in some respects we are more, certainly as far as our potential goes—in the world of the spirit 'potential' means something much greater than in the physical world—than a mere fourfold human being consisting of physical body, ether body, astral body and I. Potentially we have the Spirit Self in us, and the Life Spirit, and Spirit Man. They will develop at a later stage, but we have the seed in us. Do not think of this in an abstract way, for they are truly part of ourselves and we have encounters with these higher aspects in us. As human beings we would increasingly feel alienated from everything connected with the spirit, an alienation that would be hard to bear, if it were not for the fact that every now and then we are able to meet out Spirit Self. Our I must encounter the higher principle of the Spirit Self, which we shall only develop in the future and which in a way is of the same nature as the spirits belonging to the hierarchy of the Angels. In popular terms we might also say, using Christian ideas: Every now and then we must meet a spirit from the hierarchy of the Angels who is particularly close to us, for in that encounter the spirit from the hierarchy of the Angels does something which will prepare us so that one day we may receive a Spirit Self. We also have to meet with a spirit from the hierarchy of the Archangels because this spirit will do something that leads to development of the Life Spirit, and so on.

Basically it makes no difference if we use Christian ideas and think of the hierarchy of the Angels or go back to antiquity and speak of the human being's Genius. We know we live in an age when not many, but only a few, individuals are permitted to look into the world of the spirit and see the

realities and spirits of that world. There have been times when
people quite generally were able to see the spirits and follow
the evolutionary processes in the world of the spirit. At the
time when people spoke of every human being's Genius, they
also had a direct, real perception of this Genius. In the not too
distant past, this perception was still powerful enough to
enable people to describe it quite objectively. In the present
day such descriptions are taken for invention, yet they were
not intended as such. Plutarch, for instance, wrote about the
relationship people have to their Genius—let me quote this
verbatim.[19] Plutarch, a Greek writer, said that part of the soul
had entered into the earthly body, but another part of it
remained outside, floating above the individual's head like a
star. This was quite rightly called the daimon or Genius who
guides him. A wise man follows it willingly.

Plutarch spoke in very definite terms about what to him was
not an invention but something real and distinct. He said
quite emphatically that in other respects, the non-physical
part of the human being has to be seen together with the
physical body, with the non-physical normally occupying the
same space as the physical. But when it comes to the Genius,
the spirit that guides the human being, this is something
separate which can be seen outside the human head.

Paracelsus,[20] one of the last to have real knowledge of these
things without having received special instruction or having
special gifts, said more or less the same. So did many others.
The Genius they saw is nothing but the evolving Spirit Self,
though it is borne by a spirit from the hierarchy of the Angels.

It is important to consider these things in some depth.
There is something special about the Genius becoming visible, and we can understand this if, among other things—this
may be considered from a number of different points of view,
but let us take this one—we consider how people relate to
each other. The way people deal with each other can teach us
something that is not without significance concerning the
non-physical aspects of the human being. Someone who is

only able to observe an encounter between two individuals with physical eyes will note that they approach and perhaps greet each other, and so on. However, someone who is able to observe with the eye of the spirit will find that every human encounter also involves a spiritual process. Among other things it causes the part of the ether body that forms the head to express the sympathies and antipathies the two individuals feel for each other, however subtle, for as long as they are together. Let us assume two people meet who cannot stand each other. Let us take the extreme case—such things happen in life—of two people meeting who cannot stand each other, and the feeling of marked antipathy is mutual. What happens is that the part of the ether body that forms the head bends forward, coming out of the head, in both people, and the ether bodies of the heads come together. Antipathy turns out to mean a continuous inclination of the etheric head when two people meet who cannot stand each other. If two people meet who love each other, a similar process occurs, except that the etheric head moves back, bends backwards. In either case— with the ether body bowing as though in salutation if people cannot stand each other, or bending backwards if they love each other—the physical head becomes freer than it usually is. This is only relative, of course; the ether body does not go completely outside, but it changes position and extends backwards, so that one sees a continuation. The result is that a thinner ether body fills the head than in a person by himself. With the ether body in the head thinned down, the astral body, which remains in the head, becomes more clearly visible to the clairvoyant eye. So we get not only the movement of the ether body but a definite change in the astral light of the human head.

It is because of this—a truth, not invention—that someone who understands these things must paint individuals who are capable of selfless love with an aura around the head, which we call a halo. The phenomenon is less striking when two people meet in the usual way, with a good deal of egotism in their love. But when someone faces other human beings in moments when he is not concerned with himself and his personal relationship to another individual but with what is generally human, connected with love for humanity, the astral body becomes clearly visible in the head region. People who are able to see selfless love in another clairvoyantly will see the halo and feel an urge to paint it. These things are connected with wholly objective truths in the world of the spirit. However, this objective truth, a reality which is a constant factor in human evolution, is also connected with something else.

From time to time we really have to enter into closer communion with our Spirit Self. This Spirit Self also exists potentially in the astral aura which becomes visible in the way I have mentioned. The aura is shone upon from above, as it were, from the future. Human beings must from time to time encounter their Spirit Self. The question is, when does this happen?

This brings us to the first encounter we are going to discuss. When does it happen? During normal sleep it always happens roughly half-way between going to sleep and waking up. For people who are closer to nature, simple country people who go to bed as the sun goes down and also rise with the sun, the midpoint in their sleep roughly coincides with the middle of the night. For people who no longer live a life of nature, this is not so much the case. People living in our modern civilization can, within limits, arrange their lives to suit themselves. And when they are about half-way through their period of sleep they will be together with their Spirit Self, that is, the spiritual qualities from which the Spirit Self will be taken; they will encounter their Genius. Generally speaking, therefore, every human being encounters his Genius every night, that is, during sleep.

This is important for us, for the degree of inner satisfaction we gain from knowing about the relationship human beings have with the world of the spirit is an after-effect of this encounter with our Genius. We may say that it is the first encounter most people have with the world of the spirit today, even if it is still unconscious. People will gradually become more aware of it as they notice the after-effect. This can be achieved by refining our inner awareness in waking consciousness by taking up the thoughts and ideas presented in the science of the spirit; the soul will then develop a more subtle perceptiveness that allows it to pay careful attention to the after-effect. What matters is that the soul is sufficiently subtle and inwardly active to observe such after-effects. The encounter with one's Genius often comes to conscious awareness in some form or other, but the materialistic environment in which we live, filling the mind with ideas that come from the materialistic view and way of life, does not allow the soul to take note of what happens through the encounter with the Genius. All it needs is for people to fill their mind with ideas that are more spiritual than those given by materialism, and little by little the idea of meeting their Genius becomes quite natural to them.

The second encounter is at a higher level.

You will have noted even from the little I have told you that the first encounter is connected with the time of day or night. If we were to adapt life entirely to the natural day it would happen at midnight, but we would be less free in that case than we are in our present civilization. People would always encounter their Genius at the midnight hour. Independence has to do with a shift in this. The encounter of the I with the Genius shifts. The second encounter cannot shift to the same degree. Anything connected with the astral body and ether body deviates less from the macrocosmic scheme of things. Anything connected with the I and physical body deviates a great deal in modern times. The second encounter is connected with the macrocosmic scheme of things. It is connected with the cycle of the year, whereas the first encounter is connected with the cycle of the day.

Here I must refer to a number of things I have previously presented from different points of view. Human life, taken as a whole, is not the same through the seasons of the year, and we go through changes as the year progresses. In summer, when the sun is hottest, we are much more given up to physical life, including the physical life of our environment. In winter we have to resist the elements, as it were, and are much more dependent on ourselves. Then our spiritual life becomes more free, and we are connected with the world of the spirit, with the whole spiritual environment.

The special feelings we connect with the Christmas mystery and festival are far from arbitrary, therefore.They are connected with the date set for the festival. In those winter days when the festival is held, human beings are indeed given up to the spirit, and so is the whole Earth. We live in a realm, as it were, where the spirit is close to us. The consequence is that during the Christmas season, more or less up to our present-day New Year's Day, our astral bodies encounter the Life Spirit, just as the I does the Spirit Self in the first encounter. It is because of this that we are able to be close to Christ Jesus, for he comes to revelation in the Life Spirit. He is revealed by a spirit from the realm of the Archangels. This encounter therefore brings us close to Christ Jesus in present-day evolution, which began with the Mystery of Golgotha. In some respect we may therefore also call the encounter with the Life Spirit an encounter with Christ Jesus that takes place deep down in the soul.

If we deepen our inner life and perceptiveness, developing spiritual awareness by deepening our religious life and doing religious exercises, and perhaps also adding to this the ideas gained from the science of the spirit, we will be able to experience the after-effect of our encounter with the Life Spirit, or the Christ, just as we are able to experience the after-effect of our night-time encounter with the Genius when awake. And it is truly the case that during the period which follows the Christmas season, up until Easter, conditions are particularly favourable for bringing the encounter with Christ Jesus to conscious awareness.

Christmas is profoundly connected with developments in

the Earth organism because at that time human beings go with the Earth through the changes it experiences. This is something we should not allow to be obscured by an abstract materialistic way of life. The Easter season is determined by events in the heavens. Easter Sunday is the first Sunday after the first full moon following the spring equinox. Christmas is determined by conditions relating to the Earth, Easter is determined from above. Everything I have described so far shows that we are connected with conditions on Earth, and it is equally true that we are connected with cosmic and spiritual events in the heavens, as I am going to show. Easter is a time in the course of the year when everything that has happened in our inner life following the encounter with the Christ at Christmas fully connects again with our physical, earthly nature. The great Good Friday Mystery, which at Easter brings to human minds the Mystery of Golgotha, also means, apart from anything else, that the Christ, who has been walking by our side, as it were, during the period I have described, now comes closest to us, vanishing into us, to put it crudely, entering wholly into us so that he may remain with us for the period that follows the Mystery of Golgotha, the summer season. People sought to unite with the macrocosm in the ancient mysteries at St John's Tide in a way that had to be different after the Mystery of Golgotha.

You see, this is where we are a microcosm which in a profoundly significant way is part of the macrocosm. We accompany the macrocosm in the course of the year's life, but we are also bound to this because it is a more inward aspect of our human nature. The science of the spirit seeks gradually to reveal to us the spiritual scientific ideas that human beings are able to make their own concerning the Christ who, from the Mystery of Golgotha onwards, is alive and all present in our life on Earth.

Here I feel I must refer to something which is important and needs to be thoroughly understood by all who are friends of our science of the spirit.

It is important to show that efforts made in the science of the spirit do not replace religious exercises and religious life. The science of the spirit can be a powerful support, providing a firm base for religious life and exercises. It is important, however, not to make the science of the spirit a religion. It has to be understood that if religion is alive in us and practised in a living way, it awakens spiritual awareness within the community. If this awareness of the spirit is to come alive in us, we cannot be satisfied with abstract notions of God or Christ, but our religious exercises and activities, which may take all kinds of different forms for different people, must be something that surrounds us as a religious atmosphere, and speaks to us as such. If this religious atmosphere is sufficiently deep, it will encourage the soul to develop a longing for the very ideas that develop in the science of the spirit. Objectively speaking, the science of the spirit definitely supports religious growth and development. Subjectively the time has come when we must say that someone with genuine religious feeling will feel the need, exactly because of that religious feeling, to gain insight as well. Religious feeling leads to awareness of the spirit, the science of the spirit to insight into the spirit, just as in ordinary science insight is gained into the world of nature. Awareness of the spirit leads to the desire to gain insight into the spirit. Subjectively speaking we may say that an intense religious life may actually urge present-day humanity to take up the science of the spirit.

In the third encounter human beings come close to the Spirit Man who will only evolve in the distant future. This is mediated by a spirit from the hierarchy of the Archai. We might say that the ancients experienced this as an encounter with a principle that is all-present in world—and people also experience it today, except that modern people generally are no longer aware of the deeper truth of these things when they speak of them. It is all-present so that we can hardly distinguish ourselves from the world, for our self becomes one with the world. Just as the second encounter may also be called the encounter with Christ Jesus, the third encounter may be spoken of as an encounter with the Father principle, the 'Father' who is the foundation of the world. Here we have an inner feeling—if we get the right feeling—for what the 'Father' means in religious terminology. This encounter reveals our close inner relationship with the macrocosm, the divine and spiritual universe. The daily progress of events in the universe, the world, includes our encounter with the Genius. The year's events in the universe include our encounter with Christ Jesus. And the course of a whole human life, normally the patriarchal life span of 70 years, involves the encounter with the Father principle. During our life on Earth we are first prepared for this—mostly unconsciously in our upbringing and education, and quite rightly so—and then, between the ages of 28 and 42 unconsciously, but in the inner depths of our souls, we experience a true encounter with the Father principle. The after-effect of this may extend into the period of life that follows if we develop sufficiently sensitive perceptions that enable us to take note of elements in our life that are the after-effect of the encounter with the Father principle.

For a certain period in our life, education should be such— this can be achieved in many different ways—that the individual is prepared, at a very profound level, for the encounter with the Father principle. One way would be to encourage human beings when they are being educated to develop a real feeling for the glory and magnitude of the world, for the sublime nature of everything that goes on around them. We deprive young people of a great deal if we do not show them, in a way that they can make their own, our own selfless reverence and respect for all the beauty and grandeur of the world that is revealed to us. By letting young people experience the feelings that connect the human heart with the beauty and grandeur of the world, we help them to be ready for the encounter with the Father principle.

This encounter with the Father principle means a great deal

for our life between death and rebirth. It normally occurs in the years I have mentioned, and provides great strength and support when we have to go back, as you know, over the events of our life on Earth once we have gone through the gate of death and entered into the sphere of the soul. We can be strong and full of fortitude, as we should be, as we go back through our past life—as you know, it takes a third of the time we have lived between birth and death—if we can see again and again: Yes, that is where you encountered the entity human beings speak of in a halting way, intuitively, when they speak of the Father who created the world. This is an important idea which people should have once they have gone through the gate of death, as well as the idea of death itself.

An important question is bound to arise in view of what has been said above. Some people die before they reach the mid-period in life when the encounter with the Father principle normally takes place. We have to consider what happens if someone dies from some external cause, from an illness—which is also due to external causes—or weakness. If such an early death has made it impossible for the encounter with the Father principle to take place deep down in the human soul, it will take place in the hour of death. The encounter will then be experienced together with death. Here we may find another way of speaking of something that is always most regrettable, which is of people taking their own lives. I have already discussed this from a different point of view, for instance in my book *Theosophy*.[21] People would not take their own lives if they understood what it meant. There will be no more suicides once the science of the spirit has truly become part of people's inner life. People who die before reaching mid-life are only able to have their encounter with the Father principle at their hour of death if this death comes to them from outside and they do not bring it on themselves. From the point of view we are taking today, the problem for the human soul which is described from a different point of view in *Theosophy* might also be said to be: By seeking their own

death, human beings may well escape the encounter with the
Father principle in that particular incarnation.

The truths concerning human life that are presented in the
science of the spirit are tremendously serious in specific cases
because they have a profound influence on life. They tell us
about life in a deeply serious way, and this is something we
need in an age when we still have to find our way out of the
materialism which governs the modern world and our present-day view of the world, in so far as it depends on human
beings. It will need great strength to overcome the wholly
materialistic approach that determines our lives today so that
people may once again be able to see from direct life experience that they are connected with the world of the spirit.

It is possible to use more abstract terms in speaking of the
nature of the higher hierarchies, but we can be much more
real in speaking of the experiences human beings have—
unconsciously at first, but gradually making themselves aware
of them—during life between birth and death, experiences
that enable them to ascend through three stages: in the
encounter with their Genius, the encounter with Christ Jesus,
and the encounter with the Father. Much will of course
depend on our gaining as many ideas as possible that urge us
to develop finer feelings, refining the inner life so that we do
not pass these things by without giving them our attention,
ideas that become part of our life as something real if we pay
the right attention. In this respect much still needs to be done
in the immediate future, especially in education.

Let me present one more idea. Imagine the infinite degree
to which life can be deepened if our general knowledge of
karma is enriched by details such as this—that someone who
dies relatively early will encounter the Father principle at
death. It can then be understood that an early death was a
necessary part of that person's karma, for it served to make an
abnormal encounter with the Father principle possible. What
actually happens when such an abnormal encounter takes
place? The human being in that case is destroyed from out-

side; his physical nature is undermined from outside. This also holds true in the case of illness. The arena where the encounter with the Father principle takes place is still the physical world. Because of the fact that this external physical Earth world destroyed the human being, the encounter with the Father principle is revealed at the very site of destruction, where it can be seen again and again, of course, in looking back. Throughout his life after passing through the gate of death this gives the individual looking down from the heights of heaven the opportunity to hold fast to the thought of that site, i.e. the Earth, where the encounter with the Father principle took place. This enables the individual to have considerable influence on the physical Earth world from the world of the spirit.

Let us consider our present time from this point of view, trying to make the inner response we have today developed on hearing about the encounter with the Father principle a true inner experience and not merely an abstract idea. Let us try to look at the many early deaths with this in our hearts and minds. We then have to say that there lies the predestination, the preparation, for being able to have a considerable influence on the physical Earth world from the world of the spirit. This is another aspect of what I have been saying in the light of the sad events we have known for some years now:[22] those who now go early through the gate of death are intended to be very special helpers in the future evolution of humanity when it will need great strength to overcome materialism. We have to be aware of these things; none of it should be at an unconscious or subconscious level. It will be necessary for souls here on Earth to be receptive to this—I have spoken of this before[23]—otherwise the powers developed from the world of the spirit will go in other directions. If those powers are to help the Earth, there must be souls here on Earth who gain real insight into the world of the spirit. And there must be more and more of these. Let us try, therefore, to make the contents of our science of the spirit bear fruit. Those contents have to be presented in words and must be brought to life in us. Let us try, using the language we learn from the science of the spirit—I have spoken of this in the last but one lecture—to give new life to old ideas that are not for nothing presented again in the present time. Let us try and give new life to the words of Plutarch, for instance: that within the physical human being there lives a spiritual human being, and that apart from this, a higher aspect which is outside the head is normally part of the spiritual human being, the Genius whom a wise person is willing to follow. Let us try and gain inner feelings that may be said to help us so that we do not fail to take note of these phenomena of life.

In conclusion let us take to heart one particularly helpful inner feeling. Sadly, it is difficult for many people in our modern materialistic age to have a feeling for something that will mitigate the trials and tribulations of the present time, though they should not merely be mitigated (something we can scarcely hope for if materialism persists at the same level as it does now, for in that case it will have to get worse, very much worse). It is extremely difficult for many people today to be aware of what I would like to call the sacred nature of sleep. We see that the intellect which now rules in our world has no respect whatsoever for the sacred nature of sleep, and this is a major element in our civilization. This is not meant to be a criticism, and I am certainly not speaking of it with any intention of asking people to practise asceticism. We have to live in this world, but we have to do so with our eyes open. This alone will enable us to tear our physical nature . . . [gap in shorthand record]. Just think how many people spend their evening hours in pursuits that are entirely concerned with material things and then give themselves up to sleep without any feeling—such feeling simply cannot arise from a materialistic view of life—that sleep unites us with the world of the spirit, it sends us into that world.

At the least, people should gradually develop an attitude where they are able to say to themselves: I am going to sleep.

Until I wake up again, my soul will be in the world of the spirit. There it will meet the power that essentially guides my life on Earth, a power that exists in the other world and is present around my head. It will meet my Genius. And when I wake up again I shall have had an encounter with my Genius. The wings of my Genius will have touched my soul.

It will make a great difference to our ability to overcome materialism in life whether we are able to make such a feeling come alive in us when we think of our condition during sleep, or whether we do not do this. It will only be possible to overcome materialistic life if we arouse inward feelings that are in harmony with the reality of the world of spirit. We need to make such feelings come very much alive in us. Then our life during sleep will be so intense that contact with the world of the spirit ultimately becomes sufficiently powerful to help us gain strength in waking life. Not only the world perceived through the senses will then be around us in waking life but also the world of the spirit, which is the true and genuinely real world. The world we are in the habit of calling the real world is only an image of the real world, as I have shown in my last public lecture.[24] The real world is the world of the spirit. And the small group of people who today devote themselves to the science of the spirit oriented in anthroposophy will gain the right, and best, impression of the serious symptoms of our time, the terrible suffering of our time, if they know in their hearts that in addition to everything else sent to try us today, this is a time when people are tested to see if they are able to have sufficient inner strength and genuine courage in their hearts to make the science of the spirit, which they have to take in through the intellect and with their rational minds, truly part of themselves as whole human beings.

My intention today has been to affirm once again what I have said on a number of occasions: The science of the spirit will only gain its rightful place in human hearts if it becomes more than mere theory or knowledge and—symbolically speaking—fills the whole of us like the soul's heart blood, making us come alive just as the physical blood must be present in the whole of our body to make it live.

3. The Shaping of our Destiny in Sleep and in the Waking State

Bern, 6 April 1923

Let us look at something today that in a sense may be said to complement yesterday's public lecture.[25] I want to take a closer look at the way human beings relate to the part of the great cosmic scheme of things that has to do with their own destiny, with karma, as we usually call it. How is human destiny shaped? To answer this question in a way that relates to life and is not mere theory we need to consider the essential nature of the human being in some detail.

We often say that there are two states of consciousness in human life: waking and sleeping. But people's idea of sleep is usually just that people rest in their sleep. The view taken in modern science is that the conscious mind ceases to be active as we go to sleep and starts again afterwards, so that as far as the organism is concerned, sleep is nothing more than human activity ceasing, with a state of rest taking its place. But sleep is not just rest, and we must first of all clearly understand that from going to sleep until we wake up, our astral body and the I, two essential principles, are outside the physical and etheric body.

At the stage of evolution humanity has reached today, we cannot gain direct awareness of what the I and the astral body are doing between going to sleep and waking up. Yet what they do is at least as important for human life as the wide-awake state we have in the daytime. The I and the astral body are not able to gain conscious awareness of the complex processes that occur during sleep, the reason being that at the present level of Earth evolution the I and the astral body do not have the organs to perceive the events in which they are involved. We go through those events between going to sleep and waking up, and they influence the life we lead in conscious awareness during the day.

The best way of getting the right idea concerning the way in which the experiences of the I and the astral body influence our daytime life is to consider the beginning of human life. We have done this before on a number of occasions. At the very beginning of life, the young infant may be said to sleep into life on Earth. This means not only the times when the child is completely asleep, so that we can see it is sleeping, but really the whole period of early life which we are later unable to recall in our ordinary consciousness. A child may appear to be awake when we look at it, but anything that goes on in its conscious mind does not reach a level where it can later be remembered. Everything a child lives through without later being able to recall it may be said to belong to the period when the human being sleeps into life on Earth.

What does this state of sleep at the beginning of our life on Earth lead to? Three things have to be specially considered if we want to understand the effect of elements which the human being has brought down with him from pre-earthly life, elements he makes part of his physical existence in a way that is obscured for him by sleep. Human beings have to acquire these three things in a way that differs from the animals. Animals either do not acquire them at all, or they are more or less born with them.

We usually take a very limited view of these three things, really considering only a small part of the whole. The first is learning to walk. We are born unable to walk, and must first acquire the ability to walk. The second thing is speech, and the third the ability to think. Sometimes we can clearly see one of these coming before another in an individual child, but for humanity in general it is possible to say that we learn to walk, talk and think, certainly to think after we learn to talk. The ability to form ideas about anything put in words evolves out of the ability to talk. And it really takes quite a long time until we are able to say that a child is thinking.

However, we generally take a very limited view of the process. Walking is not just a matter of learning to stand upright and put one foot in front of the other, but altogether of gaining balance, mastering our equilibrium in the world to the point where we are able to stand anywhere, I would say, without falling over. It is a matter of placing our body in the world, controlling our muscles and limbs in such a way that the body's centre of gravity is in the right place when we are standing or walking. That is still a limited way of looking at it, however, for you have to consider that something else also happens that is of tremendous importance: being able to differentiate arms and legs.

Animals use their four limbs in much the same way—at least as a rule; if the situation is different it is easy to say why. Humans differentiate. We need our legs to achieve balance and walk, while our arms and hands are a marvellous means of giving expression to our inner life and sustain the work we do in the world. This differentiation between feet and hands, arms and legs is another aspect that is usually given little consideration when we speak of learning to walk. Here we see something which human beings only acquire during physical life on Earth.

The second thing we acquire, again by experimenting, by imitating others and trying for ourselves, as in the case of walking and standing, is the ability to talk. And it would be fair to say that talking is not unconnected with walking, and specifically the use of our differentiated hands. We know that talking is connected with specific development of part of the brain, the left temporal gyrus. This, however, only applies to people who mainly use their right hand for everything most important in life. Left-handed individuals have their speech centre on the right side of the brain. We can see, therefore, that speech is also connected with the search for balance.

Thinking develops from the ability to talk. People born

dumb can only be made to think by artificial means. For everyone who is not born dumb, however, thinking is something that develops from speech.

This particular aspect of the human being can really only be fully understood if we consider the transition from the waking to the sleeping state in later life. The situation is that physical body and etheric body rest in bed, with the I and the astral body largely separated from them. If we use the means of spiritual science to approach the human astral body when it is separated from the physical and etheric body during sleep, we find that it essentially contains the powers that have to do with human beings learning to speak. It is extraordinarily interesting to observe the going to sleep and waking up of children who are learning to talk, and also of adults who are still learning to talk, and see that the astral body is tremendously involved in the process of learning to talk. During the period when a person is in the process of learning to talk, and also later on, when he uses speech in the course of the day, the astral body takes the elements of spirit and soul that lie in our words and our speech with it when it leaves the physical and etheric body.

If you are able to observe how someone speaks, shaping words, giving his words the special timbre of the voice, if you are able to observe people putting their powers of conviction into their words, bringing the inner life of the soul to expression in words, you are also able to observe that on going to sleep the astral body takes this element of spirit and soul from the physical body and the ether body and that it holds the after-effect of the element of spirit and soul in the person's speech like ripples that continue on when it is in the world of the spirit during sleep. Studying the astral body during sleep you can see the word creations, the nuances of sound, the power of conviction the human being was able to put into his words. These are not vibrations passed on to the air, nor do they give speech a physical voice. But the element of spirit and soul which comes from human lips and is heard by human ears, the flow of speech that conveys soul qualities, is taken into the world of the spirit by the astral body when people are asleep. It is simply that this is easier to see when a child, or an adult, is still learning to talk, but it happens throughout life. The spirit and soul of what we say in the daytime is at night taken into the world of the spirit by the astral body. We may say, therefore, that above all the nuance of feeling in what we have said is taken away during the night. This is one particular aspect of the astral body.

Now let us see what the I does between our going to sleep and waking up. Initially, I would say, the I is quite naturally bound up with the limbs. The astral body is bound up with the chest, and speech comes from the chest. The I is bound up with everything we do with our limbs from waking up until we go to sleep, as we go hither and thither and do one thing or another with our arms and hands. The astral body flows into every word and when we are asleep takes away the soul aspect of the word; the I is connected with every movement we make as we walk around in our waking state. The I is connected with every movement of the hand, every time we take hold of an object. In the case of the astral body we pay less attention to the soul aspect, because speech has so much to do with the psyche, and we are not so much aware that in soul terms something very special is poured into our speech. When it comes to the relationship between the I and the limbs, we tend to take no note at all of the fact that an element of soul and spirit comes into this. We take our walking, our taking hold of things with our hands as something that happens purely as part of the physical mechanism which the human organism is supposed to be. That is not the case, however.

Every movement of a finger in the course of the day, every step we take to go somewhere, also has an element of spirit and soul in it, just as a word has. When we go to sleep, the I takes everything connected with those movements of our limbs out of the physical and ether body and into the world of the spirit. This, however, is connected with a specific aspect of spirit and soul—the fact that at any moment between going to sleep and waking up the I is unconsciously satisfied or dissatisfied. (You will understand this more clearly when we come to consider it in more detail later on.) The I feels satisfied, if I may put this in ordinary words, that your legs took you to a particular place and did something there, or that your arms did one thing or another. We thus take not only the echoes of leg and arm movements out into the sphere of sleep but also satisfaction and dissatisfaction. From going to sleep until we wake up, the experience of the I is coloured like this: You really should not have gone there. Or: It was a good thing, really, that you did one thing or another with your arms. It was not a good thing that you did something else. This is the aspect of spirit and soul which the I adds to the elements of movement it takes from the human limbs into the sleep state.

The reason for this is that when the human astral body is in the world of the spirit between going to sleep and waking up, it is destined to come in close contact with the spirits I described in my *Occult Science—An Outline*[14] as members of the hierarchy of the Archangels. This is part of the cosmic scheme of things. The Archangels are able to relate to the echoes of speech which we take with us into sleep. It is something they need and want to experience.

We might put it like this. We human beings have to breathe during physical life on Earth, that is, to have oxygen in the atmosphere, and we therefore feel that oxygen is of benefit. The Archangels who are connected with the inner aspects of the Earth feel they need human souls to bring the echoes of what lives in their speech to them in their sleep.

It is a characteristic of human speech that through the medium of the sleep state it relates to the hierarchy of the Archangels. You will recall that in a number of earlier lecture courses,[26] I said that the Archangels really are the Genii, guides and leaders of the different languages, and that has to do with this. The Archangels provide guidance for languages because—figuratively speaking, but it is so—they actually inhale what human beings bring to them from their speech when they go to sleep. Human beings immediately prove inadequate in this respect, however, if they do not bring what is truly needed into their sleep.

This is something we can see especially in our present civilization, which contains little by way of idealism. Human words have gradually acquired meanings that refer only to physical and material objects. Terms used to express ideals— which presupposes that people believe in things of the spirit, ideals being spiritual—are getting fewer and fewer. People no longer develop the élan, the inner enthusiasm, that idealism needs. They therefore tend to talk only about objects in the physical world. Words are increasingly becoming terms for objects that exist in the physical world.

It is true to say that in our time even people who want to believe in the spirit, often fanatically so, actually deny the spirit. They make spiritualistic experiments, letting the spirit manifest, because they really only want to believe in a spirit that can take material form. That is no spirit, however, which appears in a gleam of material light or the like. Spiritualism is the most extreme form of materialism. People seek to deny the spirit by accepting as spirit something that only presents itself in the material world.

We live in an age when words do not have the élan of idealism. This is getting less and less. Yet if we do not have that inner enthusiasm, or, in other words, are unable, in our waking state, to speak of our ideals as well as of physical objects, as it were turning to something that relates to the ideal, going beyond the physical world, setting goals in life that go beyond physical life, if people do not find the words for ideals in their everyday speech, if language itself does not rise to idealism, then human beings will find it extraordinarily difficult to establish a connection with the Archangel during sleep. This connection is necessary, otherwise order cannot be established in the relationship that should develop between the human soul and the hierarchy of the Archangels. If people are caught up in materialism, unable to develop idealism in their language—and words have gradually gone in a direction where people speak only little of ideals—life on Earth will be such that night after night people miss the connection, if I may put it like this, with the Archangel. They then find it difficult to enter into a relationship with the world of the spirit that is sufficiently close to enable them to live life after death, from death to rebirth, with sufficient vigour. Lacking words for idealism, human beings weaken themselves for life between death and rebirth.

It is vital to know these things. Someone who knows what it means if there is no idealism in the words we use will ultimately gain the strength to insist that idealism becomes part of human speech again. You can observe that even during life on Earth people do not gain their full strength unless they are able to absorb the necessary energy for this from their Archangel between going to sleep and waking up. With reference to the function our speech should have during sleep we may well say: To make this something we can use in life, and do so in the right way, we must really endeavour to have genuine idealism. Then our words contain not only what is needed to communicate the needs of daily life, but also a spiritual element in the form of idealism.

This emerges even more clearly if we consider the I in the sleep state. The I takes satisfaction and dissatisfaction with the activities of our limbs with it into the sleep state. As the astral body is brought close to the hierarchy of the Archangels through the echoes of speech, so the I is brought close to the hierarchy of the Archai, the Primal Powers, through the echoes of what we have done with our arms and legs in the course of the day. From the Archai we gain the strength to enter fully into the physical body, so that it does not prove an obstacle to our intentions, enabling us not only to do what is right but also to control the drives and instincts of the physical body so that we are able to achieve the goals or duties we set ourselves in freedom of thought. In our thoughts we are free, but we only gain the strength we need to make that freedom part of real life if we have the right relationship to the Archai as we enter into sleep.

How can this be achieved? Idealism creates the right relationship between our astral body and the Archangels. What creates the right relationship between the I and the Archai? We ourselves are initially unconscious during the night, but the spirit from the hierarchy of the Archai is fully conscious of the situation, taking something that is unconscious in us and developing it into a distinct idea of satisfaction or dissatisfaction with what we have done during the day. What is it that creates the right relationship between us and the Archai, the kind of relationship we are able to have with the Archangels because of the idealism in our language?

The only thing which enables us to gain the right relationship to the Archai during sleep is real, genuine general love of humanity, without bias, a genuine interest in every person we meet in life, rather than the sympathies or antipathies that evolve from something we do not wish to overcome. Genuine love of humanity in the waking state takes us right to the Archai between going to sleep and waking up. There the I rests close to the heart of the Archai, and karma, destiny, is shaped. There the judgement is made that I am dissatisfied with what I have done with my arms and legs. And from this satisfaction or dissatisfaction arises something that holds true not only for the period immediately following death but also for our next life on Earth. Strength is gained to shape destiny in the right way, so that the things we have inwardly experienced when in touch with the Archai during our sleep in a life on Earth can be properly balanced out.

If you think on this, you get an accurate picture of the remarkable connection between the I and our destiny or karma. It is possible to see, as it were, how the astral body of someone who is an idealist makes an offering of his speech to the Archangels and they are then able to guide the individual in the right way between death and rebirth. Similarly, we can see the I working on its destiny. Karma is developed in connection with the Archai. They in turn have the power to give us not only what we need to go through the period between death and rebirth but also the strength we need when next we descend into the earthly world to use what we have brought with us from the previous life to learn to walk, find our balance and learn to differentiate feet and hands, arms and legs in early childhood.

It is strange to see the effort a child makes to progress from crawling to walking, first of all gaining its balance, as a consequence of the way the I connected in sleep with the Archai, doing so in the right way because of that general love for humanity. This comes to expression in learning to walk. You can study this in detail, observing how the child topples over again and again, which is due to the fact that it developed a great hatred of human beings in an earlier life. It then only approached the Archai and did not come close enough to make the right relationship. The effect of this can be seen when the child learns to walk and keeps toppling over. Anyone who develops an eye for this, perhaps saying to himself: 'I want to become a real teacher by watching the children as they learn to walk,' would really see an enormous amount in the way the child learns to walk which it is also the teacher's work to balance out karmically. Balance has to be established if inadequate—or adequate but wrongly applied—love of humanity has been brought into this life from the one that went before.

The materialistic point of view is limited to the physical, with the human organism described like a machine as it comes upright, learns to walk, and so on. But everything physical always also has a spiritual aspect, and anyone able to see the whole picture realizes that the previous life on Earth has an effect on a child's learning to walk. Learning to walk altogether reflects the way a human being coming into a new life on Earth learns to control his physical body. For anyone able to see the whole picture, learning to walk is not limited to being able to get one's legs upright and the whole body upright, but also means that inner processes develop, including the way in which the individual inwardly learns to control his glandular functions, and so on. When a child has learned to walk, and even before this, it is not just a question of walking, but also, let us say, of whether it has or has not learnt to control its glandular functions when it has more of a phlegmatic or choleric character or an excess of particular emotions. This has to do with the relationship with the Archai developed during sleep out of general love of humanity or lack of such love.

The materialist will say people rest when they sleep. But they do not merely rest. If they develop the right idealism during their waking hours they take with them into sleep the potential for the astral body to rise to the hierarchy of the Archangels and enter into a relationship with the world of the spirit that allows them to live their life from death to rebirth in the right way. If we do not do so in the right way we will, of course, bring weaknesses into life on Earth. But it will depend on the way we establish a relationship to the Primal Powers, the Archai, how we shape our next life. You see, therefore, that general love of humanity is a creative power. For what do we need if we are to be strong and robust in a life, able to control the living physical body and put it at the service of the soul? We need to have developed love of humanity in our previous life, a true soul quality.

You will remember my saying in earlier lectures[27] that the soul aspect of one life on Earth comes to fruition in the physical aspect of the next life, the spiritual aspect of one life on Earth in the soul aspect of the next life. That is the situation I have been talking about today.

It simply will not do to speak in general terms of destiny or karma. But we can certainly say that it is possible to see how a human being works on his karma. He weaves it during sleep, but harvests what he needs for his weaving during waking hours. The threads he weaves must be made of general love of humanity. Threads that keep breaking, creating bad karma for the next life, are made of hatred for humanity. The creative powers that mainly determine karma are love and hate for humanity.

Now we have to look at this in the right way. Essentially it is easy to speak of karma by saying: I am sick—well, that's my karma. Misfortune has come—it's karma. I won't say that this would be a kind of wisdom of life designed to be reassuring, but it is easy to be fatalistic and put it all down to karma. This is far from right, however. For let us assume you consider not this life on Earth but the next but two, and from that life on Earth look back on the present one. Then you will say: It is my karma. But your karma then refers back to this present life on Earth, which is when it evolved. This means that karma is evolving all the time.

We do not have to put everything down to the past. We have to realize that to have the right attitude to karma makes us say to ourselves: An illness which affects me now need not be due to earlier weaknesses of soul, for a disease may develop as a primary event. Karma applies nevertheless. If I have an illness or misfortune in this life, something will later balance it out, or the misfortune or illness may itself be a balancing factor.

This means we must always also take the future into account when speaking of karma. Our relationship to karma is such that we become unshakeable in our acceptance of general world justice, knowing that everything balances out, but not by simply stopping the sequence of lives on Earth with the present one and putting everything down to the past.

To have a living relationship to the karmic progress of life's events we must know that there is balance. What matters, however, is the inner mood which arises from this. The inner mood which must arise from our approach to karma must be such that if something, let us say a misfortune, comes to restore the balance for a weakness of soul in the past, we take this as an opportunity to say to ourselves: If you had not had this misfortune, you would have continued in that weakness. Looking into the depths of your soul you have to say: It is right that this misfortune came to me, for this cancels out a weakness, removing it.

To wish to avoid a misfortune that balances out an earlier inner weakness or misdemeanour is not in accord with the full dignity of the human being. You are saying, as it were: It's all the same to me if I remain weak or gain some degree of strength. But you only have the right approach to misfortune if you say: If it is because of a past weakness, it is good that it has happened to me. For the misfortune will make me feel the weakness I once had, which may have taken the form of a misdemeanour. I now cancel this weakness out and grow strong again.

When a misfortune happens as a primary event in karma, the right mood is to say: If people only had what they wished, the life they led would make them quite weak. It may well be that we had a good and comfortable life for one or two incarnations on Earth, with only the things we wished for happening to us, but in our third or fourth life on Earth we would be quite incapable of taking action, for no effort would have been be made to overcome obstacles. Obstacles can only be overcome if something unexpected and undesirable happens. If we develop the right strength by coping with obstacles, if we take sufficient love of humanity with us into sleep, the karma woven by the I, which is in touch with the Archai, will be such that things are properly balanced out in the next life.

All anthroposophical truths must be more than mere theory; they must allow us to realize something. They are always such that they enter into the mood, the constitution of soul. If they do not, the individual has not fully grasped them and they have remained mere theory. Understanding karma, destiny, rightly makes people more subtly receptive for good and ill fortune than they would otherwise be—they will experience good and ill fortune powerfully—but they will also find it possible to enter into an inner mood in relation to the world of the spirit that arises not from a creed, but from understanding what the I and the astral body do when they have withdrawn from daytime life. Recognizing this, they enter into a mood where they hold firmly to world justice. To understand karma is to see world justice in the right light. It does not mean to be phlegmatic about good and ill fortune, pleasure and pain; it means to know the right place for pleasure and pain, good and ill fortune, in life.

We may well say that we only see the I and the astral body's activities in the physical body when we look at the human being in daytime life, and this means we only know something of their influences on the physical body, and nothing of the element of spirit and soul in the I and astral body. When I talk to people, I pay attention to the words they say, and if I am a materialist I explain this to myself as follows: The lung, larynx and so on are active and this produces waves in the air that reach my ear, and so on. Yet taking the right view I see the human astral body vibrating in the words that are produced and the forms created in speech. And I find that this astral body is connected with man's relationship to the world of divine spirit. I say to myself: When the astral body is in the physical body during waking daytime hours, it lies hidden in speech and similar activities. During the night it takes part in the life of the higher hierarchies. In a similar way this also holds true for the I.

We are thus able to say that when human beings rest this is something not limited to everyday life. They are at work in the world of the spirit, just as with their living physical bodies they are at work and speaking in the physical world. Materialists may deny that the I and astral body are real entities during sleep, but they also have to accept that they cannot understand the world as a whole. For what is morality to a materialist? For him, morality is something people decide on in their minds and which has nothing to do with the powers that create our world. For someone who truly and truthfully perceives the reality of human life, the moral world order is something in which human beings live as powerfully during sleep as they live in air and light in their waking hours.

There is another important aspect. When we die we take speech with us—the same applies to karma. We die, and throughout life we were more or less inadequately connected with the world of the Archangels. This happened each time we slept. We take with us through the gate of death into the world of the spirit what the Archangels gave us in our sleep, and we are then able to find our way in the world of the spirit during life between death and rebirth. That world is the Logos, consisting of cosmic elements that have their image in the words of our language.

It is not quite as simple as that, however. When we go through death we no longer have a physical body. It is enough to have what the Archangels gave us each time we were asleep, so that we might be active and use this between death and rebirth. When we wake up as physical creatures on Earth, we have to return to the living physical body. This is something the Archangels are quite unable to provide for. Higher hierarchies have to come in at this point, the spirits I called the Exusiai and Kyriotetes in my *Occult Science*. They have to bring the things we have achieved together with the Archangels through the spirituality of speech and language into the drives and cravings of the living physical body, which normally offers resistance to this. It then flames up in the voice of conscience. When the principles we bring into the living body from sleep flame up as the voice of conscience, something given by the hierarchy of Exusiai and Kyriotetes, which is above that of the Archangels, is active in this voice of conscience.

If we look around the physical world and find some people whose conscience is so highly developed that their physical bodies have better drives and instincts, the idealism in their language has enabled the hierarchy of Exusiai and Kyriotetes to work on them in the right way.

Again, if people have a general love of humanity and thus establish the right relationship to the Archai, the Prime Powers, they evolve a karma that in their next life on Earth becomes part of the body as they learn to walk, achieve balance, gain dexterity in their arms and learn to control the glandular system as they sleep into life on Earth in their earliest childhood. For we have achieved the ability to work with the Archai between death and rebirth. But if we are to achieve a subtle feeling for, and a clear awareness of, our own actions, the hierarchy I have called the Dynamis in my *Occult Science* must work together with the Archai, that is, spirits from a higher hierarchy.

People who do not have a general love of humanity, a real interest in their human environment, will not be able to make the right connection with the Archai. They ruin their chances of weaving the karma of their next life on Earth in the right way, and further lives on Earth will have to balance this out. They will also suffer the disadvantage in this present life that they are less and less able to develop the power to bring the judgements which are made—satisfaction or dissatisfaction with the activities of arms and legs—from the world of spirit into the physical body. This is something we cannot do for ourselves; increased love of humanity must bring us together with the Dynamis for this. Otherwise we fold up, even if we know what is right.

Freedom can be achieved in our thoughts. But the ability to use our freedom rightly in physical life depends on achieving the right balance in our waking and sleeping, because we must find the right way of coming together with both Archai and Dynamis.

The highest hierarchy, Seraphim, Cherubim and Thrones, want to take our activities out into the world. Exusiai, Dynamis and Kyriotetes bring everything we perceive in our thoughts from sleep into our physical nature as moral strength. The Seraphim, Cherubim and Thrones then take it out into the world, so that our own moral strengths become creative powers in the world.

If our moral strengths perform their right functions when the Earth finally enters into its Jupiter stage, the Seraphim, Cherubim and Thrones can of course only be involved if we provide a proper basis for them. If we give them powers of destruction because we are getting weaker and weaker, we play a part in the destruction of the Earth and not the development of Jupiter.

You see, the world of the spirit is differentiated in anthroposophy so that we not only have names for the different levels, but may also gradually enter truly into the whole great scheme of things, gaining an overview of the relationship between man and the world of spirit just as we generally perceive the relationship between man and the physical world. Human beings will gain the strength that will be needed for a constructive life if they find the way that shows them their relationship to the world of spirit and do not merely believe sleep exists for the purpose of rest. They need to be convinced that sleep exists to gain the right relationship to the world of spirit through the after-effects of physical life.

True, humans beings are able to deny the world of spirit and moral qualities, for at the present stage on Earth they initially sleep through it. It needs a true science of the spirit to show them what they are sleeping through. They sleep through the heavenly part of existence in life on Earth. Human beings have the ability to sleep so that they may gather the strength they need for physical life from the world of the spirit.

Consider how the aspects I have attempted to present in outline today relate to my *Philosophy of Spiritual Activity*. You will find that in the book I said emphatically that it is not a question of establishing the theory of free will; it is thought that must be free. Thought must govern the will if we want to be independent human beings. We do, however, have to arrange our lives in such a way that the will does not offer impossible obstacles to our independent thoughts. We can make our thoughts independent because of the way we have evolved in the physical world. Heart and mind and will can only be free if we establish the right relationship to the Archangels in our heart and mind, and the right relationship to the Archai in our will.

Because of this, the following is true. During the night, we let everything that lives in our speech go out with the element of spirit and soul. We also let the element that lives in our will go out. Astral body and I go out of the living body. The etheric body remains with the physical body. Thinking that is connected with the etheric body continues in the etheric body. In our ordinary state of consciousness we know nothing of the way the etheric body thinks between going to sleep and waking up, because we are out of the body. It is quite untrue to say we do not think in our sleep; we do think all the time we are asleep. Thoughts are continually running their course in our ether body, only we have no knowledge of this. We only begin to know something again when we enter into the living body; then our thoughts come alive again to the conscious mind. We are able to know freedom in our thoughts because the ether body connects our thoughts with the physical body in this way. And we are on this Earth in order to gain freedom. The power to be free can only be found in the world of the spirit, the power to be free in heart and mind, and the power for freedom in our will.

This is the connection with the fact that human beings keep their etheric body as the actual basis for thought for the whole of their life on Earth. During that life, the etheric body does not go out into a cosmic world. The astral body and the I do go out. The ether body only goes out when we die. We then look back on our life for two or three days, surveying the whole of it, similar to the way I described Imagination, the first stage of higher perception.[28] It inevitably happens after death that the human being looks back on the past life. The whole sea of thoughts he went through in his sleeping and waking hours between birth and death presents itself during the first three days after death—a sea of interweaving thoughts. Then the cosmos lays claim to them. They dissolve, and after two or three days the whole retrospective review has vanished into the cosmos. We say that the etheric body has also separated. In reality the cosmos has received it, absorbed it. It grew bigger and bigger until it finally became wholly part of the cosmos. We are then received into the higher hier-archies as I and astral principle, and can only descend to life on Earth again when we obtain a new ether body. We can then continue to work on ourselves to become independent human beings. It is the goal of life on Earth to make human beings free and independent. This is the gift they receive on Earth, the basis for freedom which exists in pure thought. It is also the reason why the ether body stays connected with the physical body throughout life on Earth, dissolving after death into worlds where freedom is not learned. Freedom is learned during life on Earth; as you know, this happens only during certain periods in life on Earth.

We can see, therefore, that freedom is definitely connected with karma, for it has to do with the part that remains lying in bed, remaining connected with us even during sleep, and does not separate from us. The weaving of karma is something separate from the aspect of the human being that holds free-dom. Karma does not work on free or unfree thoughts, it works on heart and mind and on the will. It arises from the depths of the human being, from the dreaming heart and the sleeping will. We can pour into it, or rather face it with, everything that lives in freedom of thought, in pure thinking, in the ethical, moral impulses I described in my *Philosophy of Spiritual Activity* and which must be in the sphere of pure thought.

And so everything really comes together. And it will be important for us to realize more and more that all the details come together as a whole as we progress in anthroposophy. Of course, if someone starts in a limited field he will find one contradiction after another. It cannot be any other way, because to realize that things are the way they are presented in a particular field it is necessary to consider this field in relation to the whole. Otherwise we are like someone forming an opinion on a single planet and unable to see why it moves in a particular way. We have to consider the whole planetary system. If we want to know something about the world and about life, we must try to see the whole scheme of things, physical, psychological and spiritual facts and the detailed facts in the different spheres.

This is what I wanted to discuss today, when the opportunity had arisen for the group to meet. I wanted to bring something that helps you to know the mood in which human beings can approach karma, or world justice, by finding the right, living way of entering into anthroposophy. The inner responses we develop in life are what matters, not mere understanding of theoretical aspects. May you truly grow in your ability to make the things anthroposophy is able to give not mere thoughts in your heads, but something you hold in your souls and indeed your hearts. The more you are able to take anthroposophy into your hearts as you seek to gain understanding, the more will it also be possible to make anthroposophy increasingly part of the general life of mind and spirit. And we need this sorely, for humanity will not be able to progress with the old traditions, the old things. Try and let anthroposophy increasingly find its way from head to heart. It will be safe and secure in your hearts.

4. The Human Being's Relationship to his Angel and to the Higher Hierarchies

Oslo, 27 November 1921

We have seen that in the light of anthroposophical knowledge man has to be seen in relation to the whole universe, and have first of all considered the form and configuration of the human being. We found that it related to the fixed stars, or rather the zodiac as their representative. We have seen that forces come from those constellations when they connect with powers of the Sun, and that the shape of the human head and the organs connected with it relates to the upper constellations in the zodiac—Ram, Bull, Twins, Cancer. The organization of the human chest is connected with the middle constellations—Lion, Virgin, Scales and Scorpion, and the principles that lead to the development of the human metabolism and limbs with the lower constellations—Archer, Goat, Waterman and Fishes. We are thus able to say that the fixed stars—for the zodiacal constellations merely serve as representatives of fixed star influences on the human being—have an effect on the configuration and form of the human being.

The planetary sphere influences the levels of human life. It has to be understood that we have different levels of life in us. We would not be able to think, our head would not be the organ of thought, if life were as active in the head as it is in the metabolic organs, for instance. If metabolism grows too active in the head, consciousness is lost and we are unable to think. This immediately shows that life has to be reduced, inhibited, go through partial death for consciousness, the life of ideas, to develop. Conversely, ebullient, powerful, intense vitality is needed for the will to be active, which happens at a more unconscious level.

The levels of human life thus include some that go more in the direction of death, and others that are truly levels of life, like the intensely powerful organic life we see in a child, for instance, before the ability to think develops. This childhood level of life continues in us, but life going in the direction of death gradually enters into it.

The different levels of life depend on the planetary sphere. Compared to the fixed stars, which influence human beings with their physical forces, the planetary sphere acts through its etheric powers, which means its influences are more subtle. It is a fact that the human physical body has its form and configuration from the fixed stars, not from something on Earth, and its levels of life from the planetary sphere.

Having considered the form of the human physical body and the levels of life in the human etheric body, let us progress to the life of the human soul and spirit. This, however, calls for a different approach. During the day, when we are awake, the physical body and the etheric body present us with things we can perceive with the senses and digest in our thinking. We are only truly awake in the things our senses perceive and our thinking is able to digest.

It is different with our feeling. Even a superficial look will tell that we are not as awake in our feelings as we are in our thinking and sensory perception. When we wake up in the morning and take in the colours and sounds of the outside world, becoming conscious of differences in temperature, we enter into a state of full, waking consciousness where we process everything the senses provide in our thinking. When feelings emerge from the soul, however, we cannot say that we are as aware and conscious as we are in our thinking. Feelings follow from sensory perceptions. One thing we perceive pleases, another displeases. Our feelings also connect with our thinking, but if we compare the images we experience in dreams with what we experience in our feelings, we find there is an obvious relationship between dreaming and feeling.

Dreams must be taken into the life of wide-awake thoughts

before we can evaluate and properly understand them. Feelings, too, must first be observed in the life of thought, as it were, if we want to relate them to ourselves in the right way. We are really dreaming when we feel. Our night-time dreams are in images. When we are awake we dream in our feelings. And in the sphere of the will we are completely asleep even during our waking hours. Just consider: if you raise an arm, if you do one thing or another, you know the movement your arm or hand performs because you see it; but you do not know how the power of the will actually works in your organism. You know as little about this as you know about your condition from going to sleep until you wake up again. We are asleep in our will and our actions when we are otherwise awake in making sensory perceptions and living in thought. Thus we sleep not only between going to sleep and waking up, but in part of ourselves also when we are awake. We are asleep in the will and we dream when we feel.

Anything we experience in sleep is essentially outside our conscious awareness, and so is the true nature of our feeling and will. It is nevertheless important for us to gain awareness of experiences gained in worlds of which we have no conscious awareness in ordinary life.

You know from your anthroposophical studies that between going to sleep and waking up our I and astral body are outside the physical and etheric bodies. It may become particularly important to know what the I and the astral body experience between going to sleep and waking up. Awake, we have sensory perceptions in the world of nature; we might say we go as far as perceiving that world through the senses. Our sensory perceptions and daytime thinking do not, however, take us beyond the surface of things.

Now someone may well say he can get beyond the surface. He may take the piece of wood his senses perceive, cut it to pieces and say this takes him inside. That is not true, however, for if you cut a piece of wood you merely get a new surface, gaining new surfaces each time you cut. Right down to the level of molecules and atoms you never have anything but surfaces. You do not reach what we may call the true inward nature of things. This is beyond sensory perception. We can visualize our sensory perceptions to be like a tapestry spread around us. We perceive what is on this side of it, but not what lies on the other side. We are in the world of the senses from waking up until we go to sleep, and our souls are filled with the impressions gained in the world of the senses. Entering into sleep we are no longer in the world of the senses, on this side, but truly in the inwardness of things, beyond the tapestry of the senses. Yet we know nothing of this with the conscious mind we have on Earth, and we dream of all kinds of things which are supposed to be beyond sensory perception. We dream of molecules, of atoms; but those are mere dreams, dreams we have in waking consciousness. We invent molecules and atoms which are supposed to be real. But if you consider even the most meticulous up-to-date description of atoms you find they are nothing but small items described in the mode we use for things experienced on the surface in waking consciousness. This is fiction created on the basis of experiences gained in waking consciousness on this side of the tapestry of the senses.

When we go to sleep, however, we leave the world of the senses behind and go to the other side. Here, we experience the world of nature through the senses and in our daytime thinking. There, on the other side, from going to sleep to waking up, we experience the world of spirit which we also go through before birth and after death. Human beings are, however, so constituted in present Earth evolution that consciousness is extinguished when they go beyond the world of the senses. Their conscious awareness is not strong enough to enter into this world of spirit. On the other hand the Imagination, Inspiration and Intuition we know from the science of the spirit provide knowledge of the world beyond the tapestry of the senses. The first thing we discover is the lowest level of the world which we also call the world of the hierarchies.

Waking up, we find ourselves in the world where animals, plants and minerals are, entities from the three realms of nature that belong to the world of the senses. Going to sleep we first of all enter the region of the Angels, which is immediately above the human level. And from going to sleep until we wake up we are first of all in touch with our own Angel. The connection is like the connection we have with the world of the senses through our eyes and ears when on this side. We may not be aware of our connection with the world of the Angels, but it exists nevertheless. The connection extends into our astral body.

If we were to wake up suddenly as we live in our astral body during sleep, we would be in touch with the world of the Angels, initially with the Angel who has a connection with our own life, just as we are connected with animals, plants and minerals here in the Earth world.

Even in the Earth world, we see more if we are attentive and school our thoughts than we do if we are inattentive and superficial. Thus our relationship to the three realms of nature can be quite deep or it may be superficial.

The same holds true in the world of spiritual entities, though conditions are different there. People who are entirely given up to the material world in their thoughts and refuse to rise above it, not wanting to know about moral ideals that go beyond mere utilitarian purposes, not wanting to know true love for humanity, people to whom it has never occurred to turn to the divine and spiritual world in devotion during their waking hours, will lack the power that is needed for getting in touch with their Angel in the right way as they go to sleep. This Angel may be said to wait always until we go to sleep, to see what ideal feelings and thoughts we bring with us. The more we bring, the closer will our relationship to the Angel be during the hours of sleep. We may say that throughout life we gather everything we develop inwardly that lies outside material interests in our waking hours; we gather the elements that will make the relationship to our Angel closer and closer.

And when we go through the gate of death everything we have
by way of the senses drops away. The outside world can no
longer make an impression, for it can only do so through the
senses, which have dropped away with the body. The thinking
based on sensory perceptions also goes, for it exists in the
etheric body, which remains for only a few days after death.
We see our past life for the time being in a vast panorama. I
have spoken of this in my recent public lectures;[29] it is
something we can perceive in a vision, but this has to be after
our death.

At the same time we then see this etheric body dissolve in
the universe, with the ordinary thoughts based on the world of
the senses departing from us. They do not remain. Every
utilitarian thought we have had in life concerning the world of
the senses, everything we have thought in connection with
material things, will depart when we go through the gate of
death. All we take with us through the gate of death are the
ideal thoughts and feelings, pure love for humanity, and
religious feeling in the real, true sense of the word which we
developed in our waking hours and united with our Angel.

Those thoughts and feelings play a very important role in
our development between death and rebirth. During life on
Earth we are also in touch with hierarchies higher than the
Angels, and it is true to say that when we go to sleep and the
ideals that live in us reach our Angel, this Angel is also in
touch with the Archangels, the Archai, and so on. We thus
find that we continue to exist in a world of the spirit that is full
of riches. Those riches have no special significance for us
between birth and death. They gain great significance for us
only when this world full of riches becomes our environment
between death and rebirth. The more we have been able to
give to our Angel, as it were, the more the Angel is able to give
to us by way of conscious life, conscious soul content coming
from the higher hierarchies. I would like to put it like this:
Here in the physical world we have eyes and ears; between
death and rebirth, when we are in the world of the spirit, our

conscious awareness consists in everything our Angel enables the other spirits of the third hierarchy to develop, working together with the higher hierarchies. Our conscious awareness will be all the brighter, shining with true inwardness, the more ideal thoughts and feelings, love for humanity and religious feeling we have given over to our Angel.

There will be a time between death and rebirth when our Angel has a specific task to fulfil for us. The Angel must create an even closer connection with the realm of the Archangels than before. I have presented the time between death and rebirth from many different points of view—which is certainly possible—the last occasion being the course of lectures I gave in Vienna in 1914 on the inner life of man.[30] Today I am going to look at this from several other points of view.

A relatively long time after death, the important moment comes when the Angel has to hand over, as it were, to the Archangel the ideal feelings and thoughts he has received from us. We come face to face with the world of the Archangels, as it were, who are able to receive the experiences we developed in soul and spirit between birth and death. Enormous differences exist between individuals between death and rebirth, and at the present stage of human evolution there are people who have little to offer by way of ideal feelings and thoughts and love for humanity when the time comes for their Angel to pass to the Archangel what has been brought through the gate of death to serve world evolution.

The activity which develops between Angels and Archangels is one that must take place, come what may. But there is a big difference if we are able to be more consciously aware as we follow the transactions between Angels and Archangels as the events take place which I have described, or if we follow them only in a dull, twilight state, which is the state people will know who have had nothing but materialistic awareness.

It is not entirely correct to say they experience these things in a dull, twilight state. To characterize this more accurately perhaps I ought to say their experience is that they are continually pushed out of a world that should really receive them; that they feel continually chilled by a world that should really receive them with warmth. For human beings should be received with sympathy by the world of the Archangels at the important moment we have been discussing. They will then also be guided in the right way to the event I called 'the midnight hour' of existence in one of my mystery plays.[31]

After this, the human being is taken to the realm of the Archai by the Archangels. Becoming part, as it were, of the realm of the Archai he becomes part of all the higher hierarchies, for through the Archai he enters into a relationship with all the higher hierarchies. From the realm of those higher hierarchies he then receives the desire to return to Earth, for he receives the strength to work again in spirit and soul in the material substance he will receive from the hereditary stream.

A change happens at the midnight hour of existence between death and rebirth. Before, we became more and more estranged from earthly existence, growing progressively more part of the world of spirit as we were received with more and more sympathy in the above sense, attracted by it with growing warmth—or, of course, rejected with coldness.

Once the midnight hour has arrived, however, the human being gradually begins to long for Earth existence again, as it were. And on the second part of his journey he again meets the world of the Archangels. It is true to say that human beings first of all ascend to the world of the Angels, Archangels and Archai between death and rebirth, and later descend again. After the world of the Archai they then generally return to the world of the Archangels.

This is another important point in the life between death and rebirth. People who have brought no ideal thoughts and feelings, no love for humanity and real, genuine religious feeling through the gate of death will have died a little, as it were, in spirit and soul because of the antipathies of the higher worlds, the chilliness of those worlds. Individuals who now approach the realm of the Archangels in the right way in spirit and soul have the strength implanted in their spirit and soul that will allow them to penetrate their bodies in the next life on Earth. Individuals who have not brought those qualities of soul and spirit have a longing for life on Earth implanted in them by the Archangels in a more unconscious way. Much is decided at this time, for this is when the decision is made as to which nation, language or mother tongue the individual descends into. It is also decided if this urge for a nation and mother tongue is implanted in a more inward or an outer way. It is a question of whether an individual is filled with inner love for what will be his mother tongue or placed more or less automatically into the language his organs of speech will later have to bring to expression.

It makes a big difference how people are oriented towards the language they will speak in the life to come. An individual who has developed a real inner love for his future mother tongue when passing through the realm of the Archangels for the second time will take this mother tongue into himself in an inward way. It becomes part of himself, as it were, and he is at one with it. His love will be a matter of course, a love in his soul. He will grow into the language easily and, with this, also into his nation.

Individuals who grow into their language the other way—I would say more automatically—will arrive on Earth as they descend through birth in such a way that they come to love their language only by instinct, as it were, out of inner drives. Being unable to love their language, the characteristics and traditions of their nation, in a natural way, they generate this from the living, physical body in which they exist. It makes a vast difference if we grow into a nation, a language context, with the quiet, chaste love given to those who become part of their people and language in an inward way, or if we do so more or less automatically, squeezing inner love for nation and language out of drives and instincts. The first will never take the form of chauvinism, an outer, demonstrative insistence on one's nationality, but a love of nationhood and language that has truly been gained from earlier, living and true experience of ideals, a love that lives in our hearts; this comes quite naturally and is wholly reconcilable with true universal love of humanity. Such love of heart and mind for one's language and people will never make us lose our cosmopolitan and international feeling. If people grow into their language in a more automatic way, this makes them develop a heated, organic, animal love for their language and people. This is the cause of false nationalism and chauvinist attitudes, insisting on nationhood in an overt way.

Today more than ever we need to look at everything we meet in the outside world during the time between birth and death in the light of our life between death and rebirth. For the way we enter into a nation and language as we connect with the stream of heredity through our birth depends on the way we met the realm of the Archangels on the second occasion.

For those who want to understand present-day life from the point of view of the spirit, it is an important element in life between death and rebirth when we enter the realm of the Archangels for the second time. Today we see nations all over the world harping on their national identity, traditions and language in a way that is utterly false. The disastrous developments seen in the western world in the second decade of the twentieth century can in many respects only be explained if we consider them from this point of view. If we take an inward view of life, basing ourselves on anthroposophy, a science of the spirit, we have to realize that many people have in their last life on Earth gradually made themselves at home in materialism. You are all aware of the fact that the interval between death and rebirth is normally a long one. But there are many alive now who have only spent a short period of time between their last death and birth into their present life. They had not taken up much love of humanity or feeling for ideals in that last life, when sheer utility was their sole concern. Because of this, everything that now shows itself in such evil ways in the life of the West was ready and waiting for them when they made their second contact with the realm of the Archangels.

We are only able to get a real idea of the human being as a being in space if we realize that we have to consider the human figure as extending to the fixed stars. We must also see the levels of human life extending as far as the planetary sphere. In short, as a being in space the human being draws the forces active in him not only from the Earth but from the whole cosmos. And we have to go beyond life between birth and death if we want to get a real idea of social and national life on Earth.

Observation of much that happens in present-day life shows that although there is much talk of freedom, people are inwardly unfree; the endeavours which generate such powers of decline today do not have the pulse-beat of independence in them but of instincts and drives, bringing unhappiness into social life. Seeing this, we also understand it.

As human beings come closer to their new life on Earth, they also develop a closer connection with their individual Angels. Moving towards life on Earth they are gradually more removed, withdrawn from the realm of the Archangels. While they are in the realm of the Archangels, their individual Angel is also more closely connected with that realm. Human beings live in the higher hierarchies, as it were. As they continue between death and rebirth, they have to depend more and more on the realm of the Angels only; these guide them through the elements, through fire, earth, air and water, to the hereditary stream. Their individual Angels take them into physical existence on Earth. They are able to make them into human beings capable of acting independently out of the very depths of soul and spirit, providing all conditions have been met in a previous life, as I have characterized it.

But the Angel is not able to guide to an independent life human beings who had to be connected with their language and nation in an automatic way, as it were. In that case, the life of the individual will also be unfree. This is evident from the fact that although they also develop inner conscious awareness—inwardly thinking words rather than forming independent concepts—they become superficial, unfree, with all their thinking in words. This, in fact, is one of the basic aspects of human life today, that thinking is in words. We shall also be unable to understand the historical development of life on Earth unless we progress to consideration of life between death and rebirth.

To understand the human form we must thus look to the fixed stars. To understand the levels of human life we must consider the planetary sphere. To understand the way human beings live in spirit and soul it is necessary to go beyond life between birth and death, for, as we have seen, our life in spirit and soul has its roots in the world of the higher hierarchies, just as the physical and etheric nature of human beings is part of the physical and etheric outside world.

To gain real understanding of thinking, feeling and will intent, we must not only consider how human beings relate to the outside world perceived through the senses but also how they regard their life between death and rebirth. Thinking, feeling and will intent are the powers through which the inner life initially develops. Our thoughts based on ideals, the element that has entered into those thoughts out of ideal love and goodness, will take us through the gate of death, as it were. The rightness of our first encounter with the Archangels depends on the way we have influenced our thinking, the extent to which our thinking had ideal character. It is this way of thinking which takes us to that first encounter with the Archangels. After this, once we have gone past the midnight hour of existence, our thinking fades away. For this thinking is worked on after the midnight hour of existence to prepare it for our next life on Earth. Out of it the powers are created that will be present in our physical organs of thinking in that life.

If you consider the human head and the powers active in it, you find they are not merely the powers active in the present life. Powers coming from the thinking in our previous life shape our brain. In the second encounter with the Archangels it is mainly the will which plays a special role in the human being's life of soul and spirit. It is the will which mainly takes hold of our organism of limbs and metabolism in the next life. As we enter into Earth existence at birth, this will make us more or less skilled in doing one thing or another in terms of limbs and metabolism. I would say that the inside of the head is more the physical image of the thoughts we developed in our previous life. The abilities of our metabolism and limb nature reveal the activity of newly-acquired powers of will; these may be made part of us in an inward way, as I have shown, or more automatically in our second encounter with the Archangels.

Anyone able to see the evolution of present-day life, which has brought such powers of decline, especially for the West, will develop the greatest, most ideal interest in what was active in human beings between death and rebirth, in the life that preceded this life on Earth. And the insights gained in this way will give such a person a powerful impulse to give to a humanity grown too materialistic in its previous incarnation something which now, when the consequences of that materialism show themselves in the lives of nations, can encourage people to become more inward again, finding the way to freedom, to a truly inward, that is, natural life in their language and national character, a freedom that is not out of harmony with the international and cosmopolitan view.

We shall only be able to achieve this if our thinking has the fire of genuine spirituality. What do we find in human minds today? Thoughts—thoughts about something. Speaking of mind and spirit today, people are really speaking only of their thoughts, of more or less abstract thinking. We need genuine living spirituality to enter into us. Anthroposophy is about such a living spirituality which is found when we consider the world that lies between death and rebirth. Today, therefore, human beings need to consider themselves belonging to the world that lies beyond the sphere of Earth as far as their form and configuration, their levels of life and their soul and spirit are concerned. This will enable them to bring the right elements into the sphere of Earth.

We have seen human spirituality being gradually absorbed into the other elements of Earth existence, into political and economic life. We need to have the inclination for an independent life in the spirit. This alone can provide the basis for true spirituality, spiritual substance, and not merely thoughts about one thing or another. Anthroposophy must therefore incline towards liberation of the life of mind and spirit. If this does not have its own foundations, human beings will become more and more abstract. They will be unable to have the living spirit and end up with a spirit that is mere abstraction.

When we go through the gate of death, our physical corpse is interred or given over to the elements. Our true essential nature is no longer in that physical corpse. If we go through birth in such a way that with regard to language and nationhood we have become automatic in the way I have described, living thinking, living will intent, the living spirit and soul die as we are born into the physical world. The divine human being of spirit and soul then becomes a corpse within physical Earth existence.

Our abstract, rationalistic thinking is the corpse of our spirit and soul principle. We no longer have the true essence of the human being in the physical corpse left at death, and we really only have a corpse-like aspect of the divine and spiritual world in abstract thinking that is without spirit. Today humanity has reached a most crucial point where we have to decide to take up the world of the spirit again, so that we will be able to bring human qualities again into the abstract thinking that has more or less become the corpse of the divine and spiritual, and thinking that has given way to instincts and drives, to automatic responses.

You can see how profoundly true it is to say that at the present time humanity needs to overcome abstract thinking, the soul corpse we have in the intellectual, rational thinking of today, if we want to change from being in decline to a genuine ascent again. We need a kind of resurrection in soul and spirit. The need for this is apparent from what is happening in social and historical developments today. Seeing them for what they are, we are able to say to ourselves: Anthroposophy has a mission that is eternal, a mission for the element in us that must live on through all ages. This must bring us back from an external, superficial approach, from the lameness, the death of the divine and spiritual life in us. It has to bring back this divine life of the spirit as we learn to see ourselves as creatures not only of the Earth but also of heaven, as we learn that we can only live the right way on Earth if we bring the powers of heavenly existence, of existence between death and rebirth, into our present life on Earth.

II. SPIRITUAL HIERARCHIES IN HUMAN EVOLUTION

1. Angels, Spirits of Nations, Spirits of the Times

Oslo, 7 June 1910

This particular course of lectures will deal with some absolutely radical truths that are part of our philosophy, truths that are generally still far from people's minds today. I would therefore ask especially those of you who are not yet entirely familiar with the more far-reaching issues involved to accept that we would be unable to progress in our field unless we take a bit of a leap, advancing into areas of spiritual insight that are really quite removed from present-day thinking, feelings and reactions.

It will mean showing some good will on occasion; for to provide every bit of evidence and proof for what will be said here during the next few days would require more time than we have available. We would not be able to progress unless we could appeal to your good will and readiness to meet us half way in gaining insight into these things. The area we are touching on here is one that has been largely avoided by occultists, above all mystics and theosophists, the reason being that it needs a fair amount of open-mindedness to hear what has to be said, despite the inner resistance that may occasionally be felt.

You may find it easiest to understand what I mean if you remember that at a certain level of mystic or occult development we are called 'homeless' individuals. This is actually a technical term, and to present its meaning briefly, without going into the path of higher knowledge, we may say that the view a 'homeless' person takes of the great laws that govern humanity cannot in truth be influenced by all the things that normally come to us from the place where we live as part of a nation. A 'homeless' individual, we may also say, is someone who is able to take in the great mission of humanity as a whole, and that the nuances of specific feelings and reactions that come from their native soil do not come into this. You see, therefore, that at a certain level of maturity in mystic or occult development one needs an open mind, particularly with regard to the mission the spirits of the different nations have in relation to individual human lives, a mission we would normally consider to be great and good. Out of the very soil of a people, out of the spirit of a nation, this mission develops the individual and distinct contribution a nation makes to the mission of humanity as a whole.

We want to speak, therefore, of the greatness of something which the 'homeless' individual must, in a way, leave behind. Throughout the ages, 'homeless' individuals have always known that if they were to give a full description of the character of this homelessness, people would show very little understanding. Prejudice would first of all come to expression in the reproach: You have lost all connection with the soil that nourishes our national character; you have no feeling for what most people hold dearest of all. That is not true, however. In some respects this homelessness is—or could be—essentially an excursion from which we return. Once this sacred place of homelessness has been reached, the way back is found to the substance of one's nation, finding it to be in harmony with the ground and substance of human evolution.

It has been necessary to draw your attention to this, but there is also good reason to speak now, at this very time, in a wholly unbiased way about the missions of individual 'Souls of Nations', as we call them. There has been good reason to keep silence about this until now; and there is good reason to begin to speak of this today. It is especially important because the immediate destinies of humanity will bring people together in a common human mission to a much higher degree than has been the case until now.[32] Individuals belonging to different nations will only be able to make their rightful, independent and distinct contribution to this if, above all else, they understand their nation's character and have 'self knowledge of their national character', as we might call it. The words 'know yourself' were most important in the Apolline Mysteries of ancient Greece. In the not-too-distant future the words 'know yourselves as souls of nations' will be addressed to the Souls of Nations. They will have particular significance for the future work of humanity.

It is getting extremely difficult in our present age to give recognition to spiritual entities that simply do not exist, we may say, when we look at life in a superficial, materialistic way. It may not be that difficult at the present time to agree that human beings, as we see them before us, have certain aspects that are not perceptible to the senses, invisible. The materialistic view people take of life today may perhaps still allow them to accept that entities of which we can at least see the outer aspect as a physical entity also have an aspect that is not perceptible to the senses. It is, however, asking a lot of people if one talks to them about entities that really do not exist if we take the usual point of view. For what are those Souls of Nations or Spirits of Nations, as they are sometimes called today? At most people will accept that they represent a quality which so and so many hundred or millions of people crowded together on a certain soil have in common. It is difficult for modern minds to realize that something real lives on this soil quite apart from the many millions of people crowded together on it, something that represents the spirit of the nation. We might ask—to take an utterly neutral case— 'What do modern people take to be the spirit of the Swiss nation?' People would reply in very abstract terms, describing a few characteristics of the people who live in the Swiss Alps and Jura mountains. And we would realize that these are not something we can see with our eyes or perceive with other sense organs directed to the outer aspect of things.

The first step must therefore be to admit openly and hon- estly to oneself that there are entities that do not immediately manifest to the senses, and we may say that among those that can be perceived with the senses are others that work invisibly, influencing visible entities such as the human being, acting right into human hands or human fingers. We may thus speak of the Swiss national spirit as we do of the spirit of a human being. We are able to distinguish between the spirit of a person and his ten fingers and in the same way we can distinguish between the Swiss national spirit and the millions of people who live in the Swiss mountains. It is an independent entity, just as the human being is an entity. People differ in so far as they present a particular outer appearance that can be perceived by others. A national spirit does not present an outer appearance that can be perceived with organs through which we react to others or through external senses. It is, nevertheless, a thoroughly real entity.

Today we are going to develop an idea, as it were, of such a real being. How do we set about the task of developing an idea of such a real entity, using the science of the spirit? A typical example would be to consider the essential nature of the human being. If we describe the human being in terms of that science, we distinguish the physical body, the ether or life body, the astral or sentient body and the I, which we consider to be the highest principle of the human being.[33] We know, therefore, that in physical body, ether body, astral body and I, as we call them, we have before us the human being of the present time. You also know that we are looking to the future development of humanity, and that the I is working on the three lower principles of the human being, making them more spiritual so that they will be transformed from their present low level to a higher form of the future. The I is going to rework and reshape the astral so that it will be different from what it is today. The astral body will then be what you know as the Spirit Self or Manas. Even greater work will be done by the I on the ether or life body, transforming it into what we call Life Spirit or Buddhi. And finally the most sublime task we can think of for human beings today is to transform and metamorphose the most resistant aspect of their essential nature, the physical body, making it spiritual. This will be the most sublime aspect of human nature once the I has transformed the physical body, today presented as the most tangible and material part of us, so that it becomes Spirit Man or Atma. We thus see three aspects of human nature that have evolved in the past, one that is very much of the present, and three more which the I will make into something new for the future.

We also know that between the work done in the past and the work to be done in the future to create the three higher aspects lies something else. We know that we have to see the I itself as differentiated in itself. It is working on a kind of in-between aspect. We therefore say that between the astral body, which has evolved in the human past, and the Spirit Self or Manas, which is what the astral body will be in the distant future, lie three preparatory aspects—the sentient soul as the lowest aspect on which the I has been working, the intellectual or mind soul and the spiritual soul. We are therefore able to say that very little of what will be Spirit Self or Manas is to be found in the human being today, at most only a beginning.

On the other hand the human being has been preparing for this future work by learning to control the three lower aspects in some respects and to some degree. The human being has prepared for the future by learning to control the sentient or astral body, entering into it with the I and developing the sentient soul within the sentient body. Just as the sentient soul has a particular relationship to the sentient body, so does the intellectual or mind soul relate to the ether or life body. The intellectual or mind soul is in some slight way the model of what will be the Life Spirit or Buddhi, not very much so, but still a model. And the I has, in a way, brought the content of the spiritual soul into the physical body as something of a model for what will one day be Spirit Man or Atma. Apart from negligible elements in the astral body that have already been developed into the beginnings of Spirit Self or Manas, the human being may therefore be said to have four principles today:

1 the physical body
2 the ether body
3 the astral body
4 the I at work in the astral body.

Also, as an early indication of what is to come:

the sentient soul
the intellectual soul
the spiritual soul.

This is the present-day condition of the human being in the process of evolution. We can literally see the I working to develop the higher aspects, having been given the sentient, intellectual and spiritual soul as preliminary models. We see the I working on the astral body with the powers of the sentient, intellectual and spiritual soul to develop the beginnings of the Spirit Self. We see the human being of today at work on himself at this particular moment.

Those—probably most—of you who have been working with *Cosmic Memory*,[34] a study of human evolution in the far-distant past, also looking ahead to the far distant future, will know that human beings, which I was able to characterize in outline, have evolved. We have been able to look back to the distant past and know that humanity had to go through long periods of evolution to develop the first beginnings of the physical body, then of the ether body and finally of the astral body, and then to develop these three aspects further. It took aeons, and you may also know that humanity did not go through the earlier developmental stages—of the astral body, for instance—on Earth as we know it today. The astral body developed at an earlier stage of Earth evolution, the Old Moon stage. We perceive our present-day life to be the consequence of earlier lives on Earth, earlier incarnations. In the same way we can look back on earlier incarnations of the

Earth itself. The sentient and the intellectual or mind soul developed in present Earth existence. During the Old Moon existence the astral body was implanted; during an even earlier Earth existence, at the Old Sun stage, the ether body was implanted, and before that, in the Old Saturn stage, the physical body. We thus look back on three incarnations of the Earth, with one of the aspects human beings have today developing first as potential and then in reality during each of them.

Something else has to be noted when we speak of the Saturn, Sun and Moon stages. As human beings we are going through the stage on Earth that may be called the self-aware human stage. In earlier stages of Earth evolution, during the Old Moon, Old Sun and Old Saturn stages, other entities went through the stage we are going through on Earth today. It does not matter much if we give them the names by which they are known in the East or those more familiar to people in the West today. The entities who, at the Moon stage, were at the level which human beings have reached today and are next to and above us, are, in terms of Christian esotericism, called the Angels. They are one level above man because they went through their human state one stage earlier, having been on the Old Moon what we are on Earth today. Not that they walked about on the Old Moon the way we do on Earth today. They were at the human stage but did not live in the flesh as we do today. It was merely their level of development which was equivalent to the one humans are going through today.

Other, higher spirits went through their human evolution during the Old Sun stage. These are the Archangels. These are two levels above man, having gone through their human state two stages earlier. If we go back as far as the Old Saturn stage, we find that the entities we call Spirits of Personality or Archai went through their human state then. Starting with them and following the Earth's incarnations to the present day, we have before us the evolutionary stages of spiritual entities right down to our own level. We are thus able to say that the Archai were human beings on Old Saturn, the Archangels on Old Sun, the Angels on Old Moon, and that human beings are human on the Earth.

Knowing that evolution will continue in the future, and we are going to develop our lower aspects—today's astral body, ether or life body and physical body—further, the question is if it is not just as natural for spirits that have gone through their human stage earlier on to have transformed their astral body into Spirit Self or Manas. At the next stage of Earth evolution, in Jupiter existence, we shall complete the transformation of our astral body into Spirit Self or Manas. In the same way the spirits who were at the human level during the Old Moon stage, the Angels, have completed the transformation of their astral bodies into Spirit Self or Manas, or will complete it, on Earth. They are doing at this stage of Earth evolution what we shall do at the next.

Looking further back to the spirits who were human during the Old Sun existence, we are able to say that during the Old Moon state they had to go through what we shall only have to go through at the next stage of Earth evolution. They are doing now what humans will be doing when they use their I to transform their ether or life body into Life Spirit or Buddhi. The Archangels are thus two levels above us and are now at the level we shall reach when, using the I, we transform the life body into Life Spirit or Buddhi. Looking up to these spirits we may say that they anticipate, as it were, what we shall know in the future. We also look up to yet higher entities, the Spirits of Personality. They are above the Archangels, at a level human beings will reach in a more distant future when they will be able to transform their physical bodies into Spirit Man or Atma.

Just as it is true that humans are at their present stage of existence, so is it true that those other spiritual beings are at the levels of existence I have characterized; they are real entities that are above us. Their reality is not remote from Earth existence but intervenes in and influences our human existence. All we have to do now is to ask ourselves how they influence human existence. If we want to grasp this we have to realize that those spiritual entities will look different to the eye of the spirit than do those we call human today. There is indeed a considerable difference between the entities that are above the human level and those who are at that level today. This may sound strange, but all will be clear as we go on through the next few days.

We are truly speaking out of the science of the spirit when we say: the human being of today is in a middle state of his existence, as it were. It will not always be the case that his I works on his lower aspects. Today the whole human being is coherent in itself, as it were, an entity with nothing to break that coherence. This may be different in future stages of human evolution, and it will be considerably different. When human beings reach the stage where they work in full consciousness on their astral bodies, using the I to transform this astral body into Spirit Self or Manas, they will have reached a stage, in full consciousness, that is similar to the stage they now have at the unconscious or subconscious level during sleep.

Consider the human sleep state. The human astral body and the I leave the physical body and ether body. We leave these lying in bed and are then, as it were, floating outside the physical and ether body. Now imagine that in this condition conscious awareness arises that I am an I, coming as awake in this spiritual body as it is when wide awake during the day. Even today the human being would present a strange appearance to himself! He would feel 'That's me' in one particular place, and down there, perhaps, a long way away from that first place: 'That's my physical body and my ether body; they are down there and belong to me, but I am with my other aspects, I am floating up here with them.' If we gain consciousness in our astral body today, outside the physical and ether body, we can do no other but freely move hither and thither and, independently of the physical body, be active in one place or another in the world. But we are not yet able to do this with our physical and ether body. In the distant future, however, it will be possible to accompany them from one place in the North of Europe, for instance, to another place, tell them to continue on their way and guide their movements from outside. Today this is not yet possible. We will be able to do this, however, when we have evolved beyond Earth evolution to the Jupiter stage, which is the next stage in Earth evolution and will also be the next stage in human evolution. We will then be able to feel that we direct ourselves from outside, in a way. That is the essential point. It will cause a split in what we have today called the human being.

Materialistic minds will not be able to do much with this. They cannot follow something which in some respects has already become reality in the outside world, similar to the way it will be in human beings. Such phenomena exist today. People would be able to see them if they paid attention to them. They would see that certain entities, for instance, have reached this point prematurely. If human beings wait for the right moment to reach the Jupiter state, they will then be able to direct their physical and ether bodies from outside. There are entities today that in a way have developed prematurely, not waiting for the right moment. We find them in the bird world as birds that migrate vast distances year by year. The 'group soul' which is connected with the etheric body of each individual bird directs the annual migration. In the same way a human being who has developed Spirit Self or Manas will be able to control the physical and etheric bodies and set them in motion. Human beings will be able to direct them in a still higher sense once they have developed to the point where they are also transforming the ether or life body. Entities capable of this exist today. They are the Archangels, who are able to do now what humans will be able to do one day. They can direct their etheric and their physical body from outside, and are also able to work on their own ether body.

You need to develop an idea of entities that are active in the vicinity of the Earth. Their Is are to be found in the spiritual atmosphere around the Earth. Working out of their I, they have already transformed their astral body, so that they now have a fully developed Spirit Self or Manas. They use this to work on our Earth and influence us human beings, transforming our ether or life body. If you are able to think of spiritual entities who are at the Archangel level in the spiritual hierarchies, now working at transforming the ether or life body into Buddhi or Life Spirit, you have an idea of what we call the Spirits of Nations who guide the nations on Earth. We shall see that they in turn direct the ether or life body, and how this enables them to influence humanity, involving human beings in their own activity. If we consider the different nations on Earth and look at individual ones in turn, the special, characteristic qualities seen in their life and activities reflect the mission of the Spirits of Nations.

If we perceive the mission of these spirits—they are the inspirers of nations—we can say what a nation is. A nation is a group of people who belong together and are guided by one of the Archangels. The individual members of a nation are inspired by that Archangel to do whatever they do as members of that nation. If we visualize the Spirits of Nations to be different individuals we can also understand that the different national groups are the individual missions of these Archangels. If we bring to mind how in world history nation follows nation in taking action, and nations are also active side by side, we can visualize, at least in an abstract way—this will become increasingly more real as we go on—that everything that happens is inspired by these spirits.

It will be clear, however, that there is also something else in human evolution. Let us consider the period of time that began with the great catastrophe on Atlantis, when the face of the Earth changed as the continent that was between present-day Africa, America and Europe perished. We can differentiate the periods when the great nations were active—the Ancient Indian, Persian, Egypto-Chaldean, Graeco-Latin and our present civilization which, after some time, will give way to the sixth period of civilization. We also realize that different inspirers of nations have been active one after the other. We know that the Egypto-Chaldean civilization continued to have an influence long after the Greek civilization had begun, and that the Greek civilization continued to be an influence when Roman civilization had begun to develop. We can thus see nations at work both side by side and in sequence.

Yet something else also happens. Human evolution progresses. It does not matter if we rate one thing higher than another. Some people may say they like the Old Indian civilization best, which would be a personal opinion. But people who do not go by personal opinion will say: It does not matter how we rate things; the necessary process of development takes humanity further, and later also into decline. Necessity takes humanity further. If we consider the different periods—5000 BC, 3000 BC and AD 1000—we perceive something else, something beyond the Spirits of Nations, though these take part in the process. You merely have to look at our own time. How is it possible for so many people coming from all kinds of different national backgrounds to sit in this hall, understanding each other and seeking to understand one another with regard to something of tremendous importance which has brought them here? They come from the spheres of many different Spirits of Nations and yet there is a common understanding among them. In much the same way different peoples understood one another in the past, for every age has something that goes beyond the souls of individual nations and is able to bring them together, something people will more or less understand wherever they are. It has been given the German name *Zeitgeist* [*Oxford English Dictionary:* The thought or feeling peculiar to a generation or period—translator], or Spirit of the Times; not the best term to use, but it is generally accepted. We may also call it the 'Spirit of the Age'. The Spirit of the Times was different in Greek times than it is today. People who take hold of the Spirit of our Time are driven to theosophy. This comes from the spirit of our age and goes beyond individual Spirits of Nations. At the time when Christ Jesus appeared on Earth, John the Baptist, his forerunner, referred to the spirit we might call the spirit of that time with the words: 'Change your inner attitude, for the realms of heaven have come close.'[35]

It is possible to find the Spirit of the Times for every age, and it is something that enters into the activities of the Spirits of Nations, the Archangels. To those who think in the modern materialistic way, the Spirit of the Times is something highly abstract, with no reality, and they are unable to accept it as a true entity. Yet the term 'Spirit of the Times' does refer to a true spiritual entity, one that is three levels above the human level. These are the spirits who went through their human stage on Old Saturn, the earliest period of Earth evolution. Today they work from the Earth's spiritual surroundings on its transformation, going through the final stage, as it were, of transforming their own physical body into Spirit Man or Atma in the process. They are sublime spirits, and human beings may feel dizzy when contemplating their qualities. We may say that it is they who actually inspire, or, to use occult terminology, intuit the Spirit or Spirits of the Times. They take turns at this, letting the work go from hand to hand, as it were. The Spirit of the Age who was at work during the Greek period handed the mission on to one who became active after him, and so on. They take turns.

As we have seen, there are a number of such Spirits of the Times, Spirits of Personality, who take on this function. They hold a higher rank than the Spirits of Nations, providing them with intuitions. It is always one who is in charge in a particular era, giving its signature to that era; it sets the Spirits of the Nations tasks, so that the overall Spirit of the Age becomes specialized, individualized in different Spirits of Nations. Another Spirit of the Times takes over for the following age.

A Spirit of the Times has gone through its further development once a certain number of ages has passed. We have to see it like this: if we die in our time, having gone through development here, our individual nature passes the result of this Earth life on to the next life on Earth. The same holds true for the Spirits of the Ages. At the end of its epoch each hands the reins over to its successor, and so on. Those who went before go through their own development meanwhile. The one who has not had a turn for the longest time is then given a turn again. This spirit therefore returns in a later epoch as the spirit of that age, with the others going through their own development at the time. The one who is Spirit of the Age then intuitively instils the fruits of his development, preparing him for his higher mission, into humanity. We look up to these Spirits of Personality, entities we may also call 'Spirits of the Times', though the name does not normally mean much, saying: We human beings go from incarnation to incarnation; yet looking ahead to the future we know very well that different Spirits of the Times govern Earth events as we progress from age to age. Our present Spirit of the Times will also return, we shall meet him again. Because these Spirits of Personality go through revolutions, as it were, returning in cycles, we also call them Spirits of Periods of Revolution, an expression that shall be given its full justification later. Human beings themselves have to go through those periods of revolution, in a way going back each time to earlier states and repeating them at a higher level.

This repetition of characteristics seen in an earlier form is something we can notice. If you go carefully through the evolution of different human stages on Earth as seen through the science of the spirit, you find this repetition of events in all kinds of ways. One, for example, is that the catastrophe on Atlantis has been followed by seven ages, so to speak, which we call the post-Atlantean stages of civilization. The Graeco-Latin stage or period of civilization marked the turning point, as it were, in this cycle and is therefore not repeated. In our own time it has been followed by the repetition of the Egypto-

Chaldean period. This will be followed by a period which will be a repetition of the Persian time, though in somewhat different form, and then the seventh age, a repetition of the Ancient Indian civilization, the age of the holy Rishis. It will be an age when things established at the earlier time will emerge again in a different form. The Spirits of the Times are the guides of such events.

It is the task of the Spirits of Nations, who work within the hierarchy of spirits belonging to the Archangels, to bring the progression from age to age to fruition in different nations, letting different figures arise from one soil or another, one language community or another, and bringing things to expression in specific forms, out of architecture, art and science, that are able to go through different metamorphoses and take in everything the Spirit of the Age is able to instil into humanity.

All we need now is someone or something to mediate between the higher mission of the Spirits of Nations and the beings here on Earth whom they seek to inspire. You will easily see, initially in an abstract way, that the mediators between these two kinds of spirits are the hierarchy of the Angels. They are the connection between Spirit of Nation and individual person. Their mediation is required so that human beings can take in what the Spirit of the Nation wants to instil into the whole nation, and individuals may become instruments for the mission of a nation.

We have now looked up to the spirits who became human three stages before earthly human beings reached their human stage, and have seen how they have awareness of humanity and intervene in Earth evolution. Tomorrow we will consider the Archangels who work out of an I that has already developed Manas or Spirit Self, to see how the work they do from above on the human ether or life body reveals itself in the actual productions, qualities and character of a nation. Human beings are part of this work done by the higher spirits, work that is immediately around them in so far as they are part of it as members of a nation. In the first place human beings are individuals, a developed egoity, but they are also members of nations and therefore something which initially, as human individuals, is not their fault. How can someone who is a member of a particular nation not speak the language of that nation? This is not an individual achievement, nor part of individual progress; it is part of the riverbed into which people are received. Human progress is something different. Seeing the soul of a nation alive and active we shall remember what human progress means and what human beings need to move forward with it. We shall see things that are part of development not only for human beings but also for other beings.

We thus see the human being as part of the hierarchy of spirits, and how from age to age, from civilization to civilization, entities we know from another aspect play a part in his development. We have seen that provision is made for all these spiritual entities to develop their own individual natures, and how what they have to give can enter into human beings in a living way.

The Spirits of the Times give the main guidelines for individual ages. They are able to be active in all parts of the Earth because of the different nations. The Spirits of the Times inspire the Spirits of Nations, and the Angels make it possible for them to reach individual human beings who can then fulfil their mission. The Angels, who are between human beings and the Spirits of Nations, make it possible for individual human beings to become instruments for the mission of the Spirits of Nations.

2. The Michael Impulse and the Mystery of Golgotha

Dornach, 18 May 1913

Today we will look at various aspects that may show the important mission of the anthroposophical world view to be an integral part of our current cultural era. The present period of human evolution on Earth—I have often stressed this and considered it in more detail—is an important one. Every period may appear to be one of transition if a more superficial view of human history is taken, but it has to be said that our present era is more than a transition; it is significant for the whole sweep of human evolution on Earth.

The first point I want to make is one I have often mentioned. It is that anthroposophy, arising as a necessary part of human culture in the course of earthly evolution, can be understood by every single human individual even though its initial discoveries require the fully-trained powers of a spiritual researcher.

The objection immediately raised in answer to this is that there are not very many people whose level of awareness allows them to understand the content of anthroposophy as the truth. The majority regard the findings of spiritual research and spiritual science as visions of pure fantasy, if not indeed—as we heard yesterday— as one of the 'seven sects of perdition'.[36]

Why is this? Despite the fact that most people find anthroposophy incomprehensible and fantastic, it is surely possible to maintain that these truths, although properly understood by only a few, can be accepted by many if people are prepared to set aside their prejudices.

In yesterday's public lecture I explained how supersensible

perceptions can be gained and that it is possible to extricate certain powers of soul from their involvement with the body. I mentioned that powers of thought, of speech and of will can be freed and emancipated from the body so that they can work in the realm of soul and spirit where they are developed through meditation, concentration and contemplation to enable them to enter into the supersensible worlds. All such powers that enable us to enter the supersensible worlds come about because we are capable of extricating our soul from everything connected with our bodily nature. In other words, the perceptive powers that enable us to explore the super-sensible worlds are powers of soul that are free of the body.

Even in everyday life we possess one such power of soul that could be said to have the capacity striven for in spiritual research. This is the power of thought expressed in our ordinary, natural understanding. Under certain circum-stances, without having to undergo any further training, we can experience this ordinary power of thought as something that is free of the body.

This ordinary power of thinking which every human soul can have within it today has two faces, like Janus.[37] Either it is dependent on the brain, making our thoughts aware only of what can be mirrored in the brain and nervous system, in which case it is relatively passive, since it seeks support from the instrument of the brain. Or it can free itself. Without any meditative activity, merely by pulling itself together inwardly so as to become aware of its true nature, by extricating itself from the support of the brain, it becomes a more active kind of thinking.

Both are healthy aspects of thinking available to all human beings today, for everyone is capable of thinking in two dif-ferent ways. On the one hand we can strengthen our capacity to form our own thoughts, and if we succeed in this our thinking becomes active and goes out to meet even the most seemingly daring assertions of spiritual research. But if we fail to strengthen our thinking by taking control of its activity it has to seek support from our brain, which is the instrument with which we think. In this case we can only think thoughts that can be encompassed by the brain, and our thinking is not active but passive.

The distinction between active thinkers and passive thinkers is almost more important than any other, perhaps not so much for the present, but certainly for the future. Those who can quicken within themselves a degree of independent, inwardly free thinking and can thus think actively will find that this urges them to take up spiritual research. Others, who do not want to be active in their thinking but prefer to remain dependent on the brain, will say that anthroposophical research is pure fantasy because they have no idea of what can be comprehended by thinking when it is free. They do not want to think for themselves but prefer to let their thinking run along on its own.

From this point of view, adherence to anthroposophy and one's attitude towards it is a matter of inner diligence and strengthening exercise or inner lassitude and idleness. Diligent thinking that seeks to strengthen itself can comprehend the results of spiritual research, whereas lazy thinking needs a crutch and wants to make use of the instrument of the brain as a mirror that merely reflects thoughts for the conscious mind. Such thinking is expected to run on along its own lines and will therefore have to reject anthroposophical research out of idleness. The flow of apparently scientific and intellectual philosophizing and scribbling maintaining that anthroposophical research is incomprehensible stems, albeit unconsciously, from an inner idleness in the way people think, a kind of thinking that wants to remain passive instead of becoming active. You cannot adhere to the anthroposophical world view if you want to have a good rest.

This is a true description of the state of affairs. Discussions that are not so much materialistic as perhaps monistic, which go on at length about the 'fantastic ideas' of spiritual science, are in fact fraught with an incapacity to move towards active thinking, and they combine this with the presumption—founded on unwillingness to make the effort to think actively—that passive thinking is the foremost principle to be applied by people who conduct research.

Even in everyday life you can often notice the consequences of being lazy with your inner powers. If you go to a talk but cannot be bothered to follow the argument you are likely to fall asleep and miss the very point you had been wanting to hear; or perhaps you had not even been wanting to hear about it. All those who fail to pull themselves together and make the effort to think actively, now or in the near future, are in danger of falling asleep in this way and missing a necessary step in human development. They will sleep through something that is of the utmost importance, for although they may not wish to have anything to do with such things, the fact is that behind what takes place in our sense-perceptible world there exist supersensible powers and supersensible processes. These processes will run their course whether or not part of humanity chooses to sleep through it. Such supersensible processes taking place in our present era are exceedingly important, and everything going on in the sense-perceptible world is an external manifestation of them. By looking beyond the veil of sense-perceptible events in our era we can discover the supersensible events that are taking place, but in order to describe those that are of particular importance just now we should begin by reminding ourselves that the life of the universe as a whole involves progressive evolution.

We first find human beings in their earliest beginnings on Old Saturn. Then, endowed with a new element, they appeared on Old Sun, and, having developed still further, on Old Moon. With the fourth element, the ego, they appeared on Earth, and we know that when the time of Jupiter comes they will have powers of soul which will make them like the spirits who form the hierarchy of the Angels.

As human beings advance in the course of their evolution, other spirits in the different hierarchies also progress from lower to higher stages. Not only the hierarchy of human beings but also those that are above it evolve progressively.

We shall look at the hierarchy of the Archangels, which is two levels above that of human beings. As I said yesterday, we meet with a certain amount of understanding when speaking of the spirit in general. But in today's cultural atmosphere people take very much amiss anything we say about various classes or orders, let alone individual entities, even though this is perfectly acceptable when speaking scientifically of plants or animals. Nevertheless, we cannot avoid speaking in this way if we want to deal realistically with the world of the spirit.

In the cycle of lectures I gave in Oslo about the evolution of the various races of mankind[38] I described how this evolution was connected with the hierarchy of the Archangels. Successive ages are ruled by the Archai, the Spirits of Personality.

The most important among the ranks of the Archangels have been given names which we also can use, names such as Raphael, Gabriel, Michael and so on.

We can give such names to these spirits although it is not the names that are essential. We name them just as we name other things. These spirits have a definite part to play in connection with the facts of supersensible evolution upon which our development in the sense-perceptible world depends. Through spiritual science we can quite well distinguish between individual spirits belonging to the hierarchy of Archangels without giving them name-tags. We can distinguish between them because we can see that the main cultural impulses obtaining in a certain part of the world, for example in the early Christian centuries, were governed by a spirit who was distinct from the one who governed the leading nations in, say, the twelfth and thirteenth centuries, or the one who is now governing the cultural development of our own time.

We can distinguish clearly between the civilization in our own time and that in the age beginning around the fifteenth or sixteenth century, when the chief feature was the rise of the modern sciences which appeared in their full greatness in the nineteenth century and which we cannot fail to admire immensely.

Looking at the centuries during which modern science took hold of humanity as a whole, you cannot help noticing that the work this involved was carried out by certain nations who were guided from the supersensible world by one particular spirit from the hierarchy of the Archangels. This spirit is quite distinct from the one guiding the present age that is just beginning. A certain usage has arisen in the West regarding the names of the spirits of the hierarchy of Archangels. Several of these have played their part in guiding the progress of civilization since the time of Christ, and, without attaching too much importance to the actual names, I can give the sequence of a number of them, just as you might name people who have taken part in something in the physical world. Oriphiel, Anael, Zachariel, Raphael, Samael, Gabriel and Michael have each in turn governed the progress of human civilization.

Gabriel was the guiding spirit for the age that came to an end, from the point of view of the spiritual world, in the final third of the nineteenth century. It will become increasingly obvious that in that final third of the nineteenth century another age began in which quite different influences and impulses are streaming from the supersensible to the sense-perceptible world. In the age that has just come to a conclusion human souls were chiefly directed to everything the senses can perceive and the intellect grasp, whereas in the coming age those who do not want to sleep through the next stage of development will have to take note above all of the increasing supersensible wisdom and knowledge that will come into earthly, sense-perceptible evolution from the supersensible worlds.

The external effect of this might be described as follows: During the age now ended it was the task of supersensible entities to prevent the inspirations and intuitions that can flow out of the supersensible worlds from entering into earthly life. The hierarchies had to prevent these influences from entering into human souls.

From now on, however, supersensible powers will be guided and directed by the supersensible world in such a way that as many inspirations and intuitions as possible can enter human souls, so that these souls may come to understand Imagination, Inspiration and Intuition. As bereft as was the age just past of anything inspired, of any knowledge of the spirit, so will the truly living impulses in the culture of the age now beginning be filled with things of an inspired and intuitive nature.

Fifty years ago it would have been impossible to speak of things that the necessary progress of world evolution has now made it possible to tell you about. This is because it would have been impossible to bring these things down directly from the spiritual world. Only now has the door been opened. As the time just past favoured the development of the intellect, so will the time now beginning favour the development of Inspiration and Intuition.

Two consecutive ages are sharply distinguishable from one another. One was averse to any inspiration. In the other, although mighty forces will seek to oppose any inspiration, there will be a possibility to receive it and make it the dominant feature in human souls.

Looking more closely, we discover that the supersensible powers that prevented inspirations and intuitions from flowing into human souls during the age just past were not being idle. During the age of Gabriel work was nonetheless being carried out by the supersensible world in the world of the senses, indeed within the human physical body, for during the course of that age delicate structures arose in the forebrain. This is quite true, although external physiology cannot discern it. Gradually the reign of Gabriel introduced these delicate structures into the stream of generations so that most

human beings came to be born with structures in the forebrain that are more delicate than was the case with the people
of the twelfth and thirteenth centuries.

The task of the age during which people turned their
attention to the physical, sense-perceptible world, while they
were cut off from what could be inspired, was to allow the
impulses of the supersensible world to flow into physical
bodies and develop this delicate structure in the brain.

This structure will more and more be present in those who
will now feel capable of progressing to active thinking and to
an understanding of spiritual science. In the age that has now
begun, supersensible powers will not be engaged in the process of developing structures in the brain but will flow directly
into souls where they will work through Imagination and
Inspiration. This is the reign of Michael.

Thus we can distinguish between two spirits in the
sequence of the Archangels. Gabriel, who guided human
beings in the age preceding our own, worked at refining the
structure of the brain, whereas the Archangel who guides us
now does not have the task of transforming an organ in the
human body. His task is to implant in human souls an
understanding of spiritual science. This is how we distinguish
between individual spirits who belong to the hierarchy of the
Archangels.

With these two examples I have endeavoured to show you
actual character traits of these two spirits. We must not be
satisfied with names alone, for just as we know nothing about
a person called Miller, so do we know nothing about Gabriel if
we only know his name. We know something about a person
when we can say that he or she is sympathetic, or has done this
or that. In the same way we know something about a spiritual
being when we can say that he made forces flow into the
human physical body, forces that caused certain structures to
be created in the forebrain which were then placed within the
processes of human reproduction. Likewise we describe the
spirit who followed him by pointing to his activity in helping

humanity achieve an understanding for inspirational, intuitive truths. As the power of active thinking accumulates more and more in human beings over the coming centuries, Michael will be working not so much for the spiritual researcher or initiate as for those who want to understand the results of spiritual research, those who want to take steps towards active thinking.

This transition is important in another respect as well. Because of what has come about, human beings at large are developing an organization that will enable them in future incarnations to remember earlier ones. But they must first put themselves in a position that will enable them to do this.

You cannot remember something you have never thought of. If you put your cuff-links down without thinking in the evening, you won't be able to find them in the morning. But if you have thought about them and made a picture in your mind of the place where you have put them you will go straight there in the morning.

This is every bit as true of the wide horizon of earlier lives on Earth as it is of things remembered in ordinary life. We have to remember the inmost nature of our soul, everything that is taken into the essence of our soul, but to do this we must have grasped this inmost nature in the first place. Only by schooling our spiritual faculties can we learn to do this. If we have made no effort to give thought to the essential nature of our soul in a previous incarnation we shall not be able to remember it later, however well organized our bodies may be. Human beings will be so organized as to make possible the recollection of an earlier life, but initially they will feel this organization to be an illness, a nervous state, a terrible condition, being unable to make use of it. They will be organized in a way that makes recollection possible but they will have nothing to remember. People fall ill if they have impressions they cannot digest, organs they cannot use.

Times are approaching when people's organization will make them capable of recollecting earlier lives, though this will only be possible for those who have something to remember, having learnt through spiritual schooling to recognize the human soul in its special nature as a member of the spiritual world. In any life that follows one during which we have recognized the spiritual nature of the soul we shall come to recollections of earlier lives.

This is the important turning point we have reached. To understand spiritual science means, in the end, nothing other than to have a sense for this turning point in our time.

Let us now address something else. Not all the spirits belonging to the hierarchy of Archangels are the same, they are not all of equal rank. Although they take turns in the way I have described, the highest among them is Michael, and it is he who is beginning his reign in our present age. He is one of the Archangels, but he is the most advanced among them. All entities in the universe are involved in progressive evolution, and we are living in an age when Michael, the highest in the order of the Archangels, is making the transition to the order of the Archai. He will gradually take on a leading position; he will become a leading Spirit of the Times, the spirit who guides the whole of mankind.

This is the significant and immensely important aspect of our age: We must come to understand that something that did not exist before, something that has never been the case in bygone ages, something that did not exist for mankind as a whole must now become an asset for all. Spiritual deepening, which was possible for individual nations in the past, can now be achieved by the whole of mankind.

Having thus pointed out what is going on behind the scenes of the sense-perceptible world we can say that what is taking place in this physical world is an external expression of what we have described, namely, that something like a promotion of the Archangel Michael is taking place behind the scenes.

Hitherto it has been possible for an individual human being to be an individual person, and in future this will still be possible, but in a different way. Human beings have always participated in some manner in the supersensible worlds, or have at least been capable of doing so in their inner life. But the personal nuance, the personal coloration presented by the individual in the sense-perceptible world, did not come down from above; it came up from below, from Lucifer. It was Lucifer who made the individual personality. It has therefore not been possible until now for human beings to enter the supersensible world taking their individual personal nature with them; they had to extinguish this, or they would have polluted the spiritual world.

In the future, human beings will be obliged to allow their personal nature to be inspired from above so that they may take in what is to flow down from the spiritual world. The individual personal nature will now receive its nuance from the spiritual knowledge it is capable of absorbing, so that it will become something entirely new in future. Formerly human beings had a personal nature on account of the way their physical bodies made them deviate from the spiritual world. In the future they will have their personal nature as a result of all they manage to take in and work through from the spiritual world.

Their blood, their temperament and all kinds of other things coming from below used to give human beings an individual personal nature, with some impersonal elements from the supersensible world streaming into it. In the future, however, temperament, blood and so on will less and less become the means whereby one gains an individual personal nature. People will have this through the way they participate in the supersensible world, and whatever is contained in the impulses from the supersensible world will flow right down into an individual's character. This will be brought about by the impulse of Michael who brings an understanding of spiritual life into the soul. Individuals who are striking per-sonalities will have this in the future because their under-standing of the spiritual worlds allows them to express certain things in a particular way. The Alexanders and Caesars and

Napoleons belong to a bygone age. A supersensible element did, of course, flow into them to some extent, but their striking individual note came from what they received from below. Those who gain individual personal character through the way in which they bring the spiritual world into the physical, those who bring personal character into mankind out of the soul, will take the place of the Alexanders and Caesars and Napoleons. The power of human actions in the future will be derived from the power of the spiritual influence that will flow into these actions.

All this is a part of what makes the transition from one age to another significant. But the most significant aspect of all is that it is the transition from the age of Gabriel to the age of Michael in the present era of evolution.

We can comprehend what has been said today even with our ordinary understanding if we can be unprejudiced enough to look at our time and see that two possibilities existed side by side right up to the final third of the nineteenth century.

The first of these possibilities was to create a world view based on modern science. But this is old-fashioned today, even antiquated, and no longer belongs to the character of the age. People still do it because they are carrying on what harks back to former times. For the character of our age it is appropriate to construct a world view out of the inspirations coming from the spiritual world and our understanding of them. If we can take a feeling of this into our soul we shall come to know what the anthroposophical world view means for individual souls, and we shall have a sense of what evolution means for mankind. We are privileged to become participants in something very significant.

Let me remind you of something I included in the lectures I gave here last time about the changes in the functions of the Buddha.[39] This is also the point from which I shall take my start in the next lecture.

I would like to close with a kind of question, a question that can arise in every heart and mind and will take us on from the important matters discussed today to matters that are even more important.

When Michael has been promoted, when he has become the leading spirit of western culture, who will then take his place? The position has to be filled. In our hearts we are likely to assume that an Angel will also have been promoted and will have entered the ranks of the Archangels. Which Angel is this?

Closing with this question I open up the way for even more important considerations the day after tomorrow.

Today it was my intention to show you the most important aspect of the transition: the fact that individuals who make sufficient effort will be able to reach an understanding of supersensible truths. This is what the universal powers who guide the evolution of mankind desire. The image of this transition in the world of the senses is the fact that individual personal natures take on an entirely new nuance. Whereas in the past it was temperament and blood that coloured the individual personal character from below, in future the element of spiritual understanding will set the tone for individual personal nature in the new age.

It is important to understand this, and even more important to get a feeling for it.

3. Spiritual Entities Seen through the Ages

Dornach, 4 January 1924

We do not usually consider how different the thoughts of people who considered themselves to have knowledge were even a relatively short time ago in history—very different to what our thoughts are today. Today we speak of chemical substances, 70 or 80 chemical substances, and do not realize that it really means very little to call a substance oxygen, nitrogen, and so on. Oxygen only exists under specific conditions as regards temperature and other conditions of life on Earth. Surely no one in their right senses would consider something to be real which has one form and is present in one particular amount under the conditions in which humans live on Earth, but is no longer the same, nor present in the same amount, once the temperature is raised by a number of degrees.

In the middle medieval period scientists certainly had ideas that tended to go beyond the relative nature of existence and took them to true existence. I would say the transition came between the ninth and tenth centuries. Before this, people took a much more spiritual view of things. Someone who had real knowledge in the ninth century, for instance, would never have thought that Angels, Archangels or Seraphim are not just as real as the physical human beings we are able to see with our eyes. You will find that before the tenth century those who had knowledge would definitely speak of the spiritual beings, the 'intelligences', as they were called, in the cosmos just as they would of the life forms we meet in the street, though they were aware that the time had passed when this was the general view taken by people. They knew that under special conditions the effect would be there.

We must not fail to realize, for instance, that until the ninth or tenth century many Catholic priests were fully aware, at the offertory during mass, that one action or another they performed as part of this made them encounter spiritual entities, intelligences, from the cosmos.

In the course of the ninth and tenth centuries human awareness of the direct connection with the true intelligences in the universe vanished. People increasingly thought only of the elements of the cosmos, of earth as the solid element, water as the fluid element, air as the gaseous element, and the principle of heat or fire. Where people had once spoken of cosmic intelligences that regulate the movements of the planets, taking them past the fixed stars, and so on, attention now focused on the immediate surroundings in life on Earth. People would speak of the elements of earth, water, air and fire. They did not refer to chemical elements as we know them today; that is something which came much later. But you see, you would be having completely the wrong idea if you were to think that in the thirteenth and fourteenth centuries, and in a sense until the eighteenth century, even those who had knowledge would have considered heat, air, water and earth to be what people consider them to be today. Today heat is merely considered a condition in which bodies are. No one any longer speaks of the warmth ether as such. Air and water have become highly abstract in modern-day thinking, and it really is necessary for us to enter deeply into the way these things were seen in the past. Let me give you a picture, therefore, of how those who had knowledge in that earlier period would have spoken, more or less.

Writing my *Occult Science*[14] I found it necessary to present Earth evolution in a light that at least to some extent is in harmony with common ideas today. In the thirteenth or twelfth century it would have been possible to do this differently. Then one particular chapter of *Occult Science* might have been as follows. Initially it would have been necessary to create an idea of the entities we may call the spirits of the First

Hierarchy: Seraphim, Cherubim and Thrones. The Seraphim would have been characterized as spirits for whom there is neither subject nor object, for subject and object would be one. They would not say: 'There are objects outside me,' but: 'The world is, and I am the world, and the World is I.' They would only know of themselves, and this would be because of an experience of which we human beings have a faint echo when we come across something that kindles ardent enthusiasm in us.

It can be quite difficult to get modern people to understand what ardent enthusiasm is. As late as the early nineteenth century, people had a better idea of this than we have today. It could still happen in those days that people responded so enthusiastically to a poet reading from his works that—forgive me, but this is really how it was—a modern individual would say: 'They've all gone mad!' They could be stirred to such an extent, with warmth entering into their hearts. Today you freeze to death, especially concerning matters you think people should get enthusiastic about.

This element of enthusiasm was to be found particularly in Central and Eastern Europe, and to get an idea of the inner life of the Seraphim we have to imagine enthusiasm raised to the level of conscious awareness, as an integral element of consciousness. The element of consciousness of the Cherubim has to be perceived as utterly tranquil, filled with light, so that thought immediately is light, everything is illumined. And the element the Thrones have is something that sustains the worlds out of grace.

This is merely an outline. I could continue on the subject for a long time. I merely wanted to show you how people would have attempted to characterize the essence of the spirits in the First Hierarchy. They would have said: 'The Seraphim, Cherubim and Thrones act in concord in such a way that the Thrones establish a core (see drawing, centre, reddish violet); the Cherubim let their own light-filled nature flow from this core (yellow ring). The Seraphim envelop the whole in a

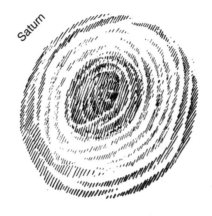

mantle of enthusiasm that shines out far and wide in cosmic space (red mantle).'

All these spiritual beings float through one another, act, think, will and feel in one another. If an entity with the necessary inner powers of perception had travelled through the space where the Thrones had established the core, the Cherubim a surrounding area and the Seraphim a kind of closing off from the outside, this entity would have experienced different degrees of warmth in places—greater warmth in one place and less in another. All this would be in soul and spirit, however, and be such that the inner experience would at the same time also be physical experience in our human senses, so that you would really feel as you do when you are in a heated room. This is how the spirits of the First Hierarchy once came together in the universe, creating Saturn existence. The warmth is nothing in itself; it merely brings to expression that these spirits are present.

Let me use an image that may help to clarify the matter. Imagine you like someone. You feel his presence gives you warmth. Now imagine someone who sees everything in utterly abstract terms were to come along and say: 'Well, the person does not really interest me; I'll imagine he's not there; I am only interested in the warmth he gives.' But he would actually not be saying, 'I am only interested in the warmth he gives,' but 'I am altogether only interested in the warmth'. He would be talking nonsense, of course, for if the person who gives the warmth is no longer there, the warmth, too, will have gone. The warmth is altogether something that is only present where the human being is present. It is nothing in itself. The person has to be there for the warmth to be there. And in the same way the Seraphim, Cherubim and Thrones have to be there; otherwise there would be no warmth. The warmth merely brings them to revelation.

You see, this truly existed at the time I am speaking of, even in the form of coloured drawings. People would speak of the elements, the element of warmth, for instance, and know that these were in fact the Cherubim, Seraphim and Thrones. This was the Saturn state of existence.

They would then take this further and say to themselves: 'Only the Seraphim, Cherubim and Thrones have the power to create such a thing in the cosmos. Only this, the highest hierarchy, is able to do so. When the highest hierarchy had created such a thing at the point of origin of an evolving world, evolution could proceed. The sons of the Seraphim, Cherubim and Thrones, as it were, could then take evolution further.' And the spirits of the Second Hierarchy, the Kyriotetes, Dynamis and Exusiai, who were the offspring of the Seraphim, Cherubim and Thrones, really did enter into the Saturnine space created in Saturnine warmth by the First Hierarchy. The younger—cosmically younger—spirits entered into this. How did they work? The Cherubim, Seraphim and Thrones had come to revelation in the element of warmth. The spirits of the Second Hierarchy revealed themselves in the element of light. Here (red background in the drawing) the Saturnine principle is dark, providing warmth. And within the dark world of Saturn existence arose

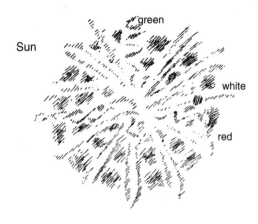

what can arise through the sons of the First Hierarchy, through Exusiai, Dynamis and Kyriotetes.

As the Second Hierarchy entered into the sphere of Saturn warmth, light shone within it. This went hand in hand with a condensation of warmth. Air arose within an element that had been warmth only. You have to understand, of course, that these were spirits entering. For someone with the appropriate ability to perceive, light entered. Light marked the paths of those spirits. If light reaches a place, shadows will arise under certain conditions and darkness is created. The entrance of the Second Hierarchy in the form of light also created shadow. What was this shadow? Air. And until the fifteenth and sixteenth century people really knew what air was. Today we merely know that it consists of oxygen, nitrogen, and so on, which is really saying no more than someone knowing that a watch is made of glass and silver, which does not really tell us anything about the watch. We do not say anything about the air as a cosmic phenomenon if we say it consists of oxygen and nitrogen; but it says much about air if people know that in cosmic terms air is the shadow of light.

As the Second Hierarchy entered into the Saturnine warmth, therefore, light entered (white rays) and air as the shadow of light (green wavy lines). And when this arose, the Sun was there. This, then, would no doubt have been how people spoke in the thirteenth and twelfth centuries.

To continue with the story, further development was guided by the Archai, Archangels and Angels, the sons of the Second Hierarchy. They brought something new into the luminous element brought in by the Second Hierarchy with its shadow of airy darkness. This was not the indifferent, neutral darkness of Saturn, which had been mere absence of light, but a darkness that brought out the contrast to light. The Third Hierarchy now brought in an element similar to our wishes, drives and desires to gain something, to long for something.

What happened then was that, let us say, an Archai or angelic spirit would enter here (see dot on light of ray on the right side of the drawing) and meet with an element of light, a place of light, I'd say. Being receptive to this light it would be given an urge, a desire, for darkness. The angelic spirit would bring light into the darkness. These spirits became messengers, mediators between light and darkness. The result was that a principle which hitherto had only been luminous with light and had its shadows of airy darkness, now began to scintillate in all colours, with light appearing in the darkness and darkness in the light. The Third Hierarchy created the magic of colour out of light and darkness.

We actually have some historical documentation for this. In the time of Aristotle,[40] people still knew, if they asked themselves within the mysteries, where colours came from and that the spirits of the Third Hierarchy were involved with them. In his *Harmony of Colours*[41] he said that colour signified light and darkness working together. This spiritual vision, in which the spirits of the Second Hierarchy were perceived behind the light and its shadow, behind darkness, and the spirits of the Third Hierarchy behind colours flashing up, the whole being part of the great cosmic scheme of things, has been lost. Nothing has remained but Newton's unfortunate theory of colour. Initiates would smile about it until the eighteenth century, but it became an article of faith for physicists.

To speak in terms of Newton's theory of colours, one no longer needs to have knowledge of the world of the spirit. Someone who still felt inwardly goaded by the world of the spirit, as Goethe did, would resist the theory. Such a person would present the matter in the right way and might become quite abusive. Goethe was never more abusive than he was with reference to Newton; he complained like anything about such nonsense. Today it is difficult to understand this, for the simple reason that anyone not accepting Newton's theory of colour looks a fool in the eyes of physicists. In Goethe's day it was different; he was not completely on his own. He was on his own in making these things public, but those who had knowledge, even in the late eighteenth century, certainly knew how colour wells up in the realm of the spirit.

Now you see, air is the shadow of light. And just as dark shadows appear when light arises under certain conditions, so does something else appear when colour arises. If colour acts as a principle that has reality—it was able to do so for as long as it entered into the airy element—and if it is not mere reflection but reality itself as it scintillates and is active in the airy element, then the fluid, watery element arises from that colour reality, just as under certain conditions pressure gives rise to counter pressure. In cosmic terms air is the shadow of light and water the reflection, the creation, of the colour principle.

You will say you cannot understand this. But try, just for once, to grasp the nature of colour in its true sense.

The colour red—well, do you think it is really the neutral surface we usually see? If you think about it, red is a colour that attacks. I have often said this. You want to run away from red, it repulses us. Blue-violet is something you want to run after, it keeps running away from us, getting deeper and

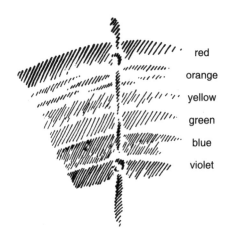

red
orange
yellow
green
blue
violet

deeper. Everything that lives is to be found in the colours. They are a world, and the soul element feels that it has to move when it enters into the world of colour, it cannot do other than move if it enters into colour with feeling.

Look at the way people stare dumbly at a rainbow today. If we have some power of perceiving in images as we look at a rainbow, we see elemental spirits developing tremendous activity within it. They produce some strange phenomena. Here (red and yellow) you see certain elemental spirits continually emerging from the rainbow. They move in that direction. The moment they come to the lower part of the green they are absorbed. You see them vanish (in green and blue). They emerge again on the other side. Seen with the eye capable of vision in images the whole rainbow shows spiritual principles streaming out and vanishing again. It is a kind of spiritual cylindrical roller. At the same time one notices that the spirits show great fear as they stream out, and tremendous, invincible courage as they enter. When you look at the reddish yellow, fear is streaming out; when you look at the blue-violet, you get the feeling: nothing but courage is alive there.

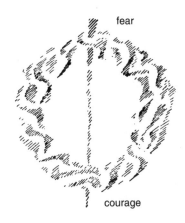

fear

courage

Now imagine that you don't only have the rainbow there but, if I draw a section and the rainbow is in this position (turned through a 90° angle), spirits emerge here and vanish here; here fear, here courage. The courage vanishes again. With the eye looking in a direction where the red is here, the yellow, and so on, the rainbow gains density. And you can really see how a watery element arises. Spiritual beings live in this who really are a kind of reflection of the Third Hierarchy.

This is something you have to know if you wish to understand those who had knowledge in the eleventh, twelfth and thirteenth centuries. You would not even be able to understand those who came later, St Albertus Magnus,[42] for example, if you read his works with the kind of knowledge people have today. You have to read his works knowing that, to him, such spiritual elements were still real. This will enable you to understand the way he used words, the way he expressed himself.

This is how air and water appear as a reflection of the hierarchies. The Second Hierarchy entered in the form of light, the Third in the form of colour. With this, the Old Moon existence had been reached.

Now the Fourth Hierarchy—I am presenting this the way people would think in the twelfth and thirteenth century, when it was still much spoken of—the Fourth Hierarchy is the human being. Man is the Fourth Hierarchy. But people did not think of this hierarchy as the two-legged, ageing, highly peculiar creature walking around on Earth—for present-day man seemed a very peculiar creature to those who really had knowledge. They would speak of original man, before the Fall, who still had power over the Earth, just as Angels, Archangels and Archai had power over the Old Moon existence, the Second Hierarchy over the Old Sun existence, and the First Hierarchy over the Old Saturn existence. They would speak of man as he first existed on Earth, and in that respect it was possible to speak of a Fourth Hierarchy. With this hierarchy came something that was a gift from the higher hierarchies, something that had initially been in their possession, something they looked after, though they did not need it themselves—life. Life entered into the scintillating world of colour which I have briefly presented to you.

You will ask if things did not have life before that. This is something you can discover for yourselves if you consider the human being. Your I and your astral body do not have life, yet they have essence. Life only begins when we come to the ether body, which is an outer, enveloping element. In the same way life only came after the Old Moon existence, entering into the evolution that belongs to the Earth. The scintillating world of colours was filled with life. Not only did Angels, Archangels and so on now develop the longing to bring darkness into light and light into darkness, which created the play of colours in the planet. Something new came, with the play of colours becoming inner experience and inner activity. It was the experience of weakness, laxity when darkness inwardly predominated over light, and of activity when light predominated over darkness. For what happens when you walk? Light prevails over darkness in you. If you sit about in a lazy way, darkness prevails over light in you. Soul colours are active, scintillating in you. This began when man, the Fourth Hierarchy, arrived on the scene. It was the moment in cosmic evolution when the powers stirring in the scintillating colours began to gain contour. Life, inwardly rounding colours off, creating angles and edges, brought the solid, crystalline element into existence. With this, the Earth existence had been reached.

These things which I have presented to you were really the basic truths of medieval alchemists, occultists, Rosicrucians and so on. They had their flowering period from the ninth, tenth to the fourteenth, fifteenth centuries. Some followed later, until the eighteenth and even the early nineteenth century, but they were considered eccentrics. After this, these things became completely obscured.

The modern way of looking at things has led to the following, however. Imagine this is a person. I lose all interest in the person, merely taking his clothes and putting them on a hat-and-coat stand with a head-shaped knob at the top. This

is the person. What do I care that something like this can be inside those clothes—that (hat-and-coat stand) is the person! You see, this is what happened with regard to the natural elements. It does not interest people that the First Hierarchy is behind warmth or fire, the Second Hierarchy behind light and air, the Third behind the 'chemical ether', as it is called, colour ether, etc., and water, and the Fourth Hierarchy, man, behind the element of life and the Earth. Let's simply have a clothes stand and put the garments on it. That would be Scene 1.

Scene 2 begins in the Kantian way. Having the hat-and-coat stand with the garments on it we begin to philosophize as to what might be the thing in itself where these garments are concerned. And we discover that this thing in itself cannot be known and perceived. Very astute! Of course, if you first take the person away, leaving the hat-and-coat stand with the garments, philosophizing on those garments will lead to pretty speculations. So you have your hat-and-coat stand, and the garments on it, and you philosophize—either the Kantian way, saying that the thing in itself cannot be known; or the Helmholtz way,[43] saying that the garments cannot have a shape in themselves and there must be masses of tiny moving grains of dust, atoms, inside them; these reach a boundary and that is how the garments gain their shape.

This is how thinking went in later times. It is, however, abstract, shadowy thinking. It is the thinking we live with today; it shapes the whole of our view of ordinary science. And this is all the more so if we refuse to admit that we think in terms of atoms. For it will be a long time before people admit there is no need to dream of the whirling dance of atoms in those garments and put people into them again. This is what has to be attempted in bringing the science of the spirit to life again.

Today I wanted to give you some pictures to show how people thought in the past; things that can still be read in their writings, but have faded away. Because they have faded, however, interesting things tend to happen. A Scandinavian chemist,[44] for instance, reprinted a passage from the works of Basilius Valentinus,[45] looking at it in the light of modern chemical knowledge. And of course he could do no other—because thinking as a chemist today you think of a laboratory with retorts and other instruments, carrying out experiments in the modern way—but say that Basilius Valentinus had written nonsense. In fact, however, Valentinus was writing about embryology, presenting it in the form of images. If you simply approach this from the modern point of view, you think it is a laboratory experiment, and this makes it nonsense. For unless you are someone like Wagner[46]—who, of course, was still taking the point of view of earlier centuries—you cannot do embryology like that.

III. SPIRITUAL HIERARCHIES AS COSMIC REALITY

1. The Third and Second Hierarchies

Helsingfors, 6 April 1912

In the last lecture[47] we saw that it is possible for human beings to rise above themselves, overcoming their particular egotistical interests and concerns. This takes them into a sphere where they first of all find their own guide who can give them an idea of the spirits we call the Angels in western esoteric terminology. We also saw that going further along this road it is possible to get to know the spirits of tribes and nations, whom we called Archangels. It is also possible to discover the Spirits of the Times, the Archai, who are active in the processes of civilisation. Taking this road, of which I gave a rough outline yesterday, you can get a feeling for what is meant by the spirits of the Third Hierarchy. For a long time you will merely have a kind of feeling for them, even if you are progressing in occult development. But when you have gone through all the feelings and inner responses I mentioned yesterday for a long time, doing so with patience and perseverance, the time will come when clairvoyant vision, as we may call it, of the spirits of the Third Hierarchy will develop.

Continuing along this road you will gradually educate yourself to develop a different state of conscious awareness, and this will bring the beginning of clairvoyant vision of the Third Hierarchy. This different state of consciousness may be compared to sleep, in the first place because in this state the human I and astral body experience themselves as free of the physical and etheric bodies. This is an inner feeling you have to develop. You must gradually learn what it means not to see with your eyes, hear with yours ears, think with the brain-bound intellect. The state differs from ordinary sleep in that we are not unconscious but perceive spiritual entities around us. Initially this is a dim awareness of their presence, but, as I said, clairvoyant consciousness will then light up and you gain living perceptions of the spirits of the Third Hierarchy and their offspring, the nature spirits.

To characterize this more clearly, we may say that someone who reaches this level of occult development will first of all really see a kind of division between ordinary consciousness and this new state of consciousness. Like the distinction which exists between waking and sleeping, a distinction arises between the state of consciousness where you see with your ordinary eyes, hear with your ordinary ears, think with your ordinary mind, and the clairvoyant state, where none of the things we perceive in our ordinary state of consciousness remain, and you find yourself in a different world, the world of the Third Hierarchy and its offspring. The first thing you learn to do is to recall the experiences made in this different state of consciousness when you are in your ordinary state of consciousness.

It is therefore possible to identify the exact stage in occult development when a person is able to alternate between ordinary consciousness, when he sees, hears and thinks in the normal way like other people, and another state of con- sciousness which in a way can be brought on arbitrarily, when he perceives the spiritual world of the Third Hierarchy around himself. And just as we are able to recall a dream when in our normal state of consciousness, he would then be able to recall what he has experienced in the clairvoyant state. He would be able to speak of this, representing it in terms of ordinary concepts and ideas. A clairvoyant who is in the normal state of consciousness and wants to know of the world of the spirit, or speak of it, must therefore recall what he has experienced in his other, clairvoyant state of consciousness. A clairvoyant at this level of development can only know of the spirits we have called the spirits of the Third Hierarchy and their offspring. He would know nothing as yet of higher worlds. To do so, he must achieve a higher level of clairvoyance.

This higher level is achieved by doing above all the exercises I have described in my book *Knowledge of the Higher Worlds*,[16] the observation of plants, animals, and so on. At this new level of clairvoyance the individual not only has two states of consciousness, being able to recall clairvoyant experiences when in his normal state of consciousness, but is also able to perceive worlds of spirit, spiritual entities and realities when in his normal state of consciousness, looking at the objects in the world around him through his eyes. He is then able, as it were, to bring clairvoyance into his normal state of consciousness, and see the spiritual entities and powers that lie hidden at a deeper level, as if behind a veil, behind the creatures and objects he sees in the world around him.

We ask ourselves what has happened to a clairvoyant who is thus in a position where he not only has to recall the events of another state of consciousness but is also able to have clairvoyant experiences in his everyday state of consciousness. Someone who has advanced to the first stage of clairvoyance can only use the astral body to look into the world of the spirit. At the second stage, which I have just described, the clairvoyant is able to use the ether body. This enables him to look into a world of the spirit when in his ordinary state of consciousness. Someone who learns to use his ether body as an instrument of clairvoyance will gradually be able to perceive everything connected with the spirits of the Second Hierarchy in that other world.

One must not remain at the level where one merely perceives one's own ether body, as we may put it. Someone who advances to the second stage makes the specific discovery that he is going out of himself, as it were, and feels no longer enclosed within his skin. With a plant, let us say, an animal, or another person, he feels as if something of himself is in that other entity. It feels as if he has entered deeply into the other entity. In our normal state of consciousness and at the first stage of clairvoyance we are still able to say, in a way: I am here, the entity I perceive is there. At the second stage of clairvoyance we are no longer able to say this. All we can say is: We ourselves are where the entity we perceive is. It is as if we put out our own ether body like tentacles in all directions, entering into and absorbing the beings we perceive in that state with our own essential being.

We know a particular feeling in our ordinary state of consciousness that can give us a notion of the experience gained at the second stage of clairvoyance, though this is of course infinitely more intense, being not just a feeling but enhanced to the level of perception, understanding, and finally of entering into the other. The feeling we ordinarily know is compassion and love. If we reflect on the nature of compassion and love—something of this has already been mentioned yesterday—we find they help us to be free of ourselves and to enter into the other in a living way. It is truly a beautiful mystery in human life that we are able to experience compassion and love. Hardly anything we know in our ordinary state of consciousness can convince us of the divine nature of existence as does our potential for love and compassion. We normally experience our own existence in ourselves, or we experience the world as we perceive it through the senses or grasp it with the intellect. No eye and no intellect is able to look into a human heart and soul, for it keeps its pain and pleasures closely guarded. And we ought to realize how beautiful and mysterious it is that we are able to pour ourselves, as it were, into the essential life and reality of the other soul with its pleasures and pain.

Someone who has reached the second stage of clairvoyance learns to enter not only into all that has conscious awareness, into everything that can suffer and experience joy in a human way or resembling the human way, but also into all that lives. Please note, I am saying 'all that lives'. At this second stage the clairvoyant learns to enter into all that lives, not yet into the mineral world around us which seems dead and lifeless to us. Entering into living things also involves perceiving what goes on in the inner life of others. We feel ourselves to be inside living entities, we learn to live with the plants, with the animals, with other people at this stage of clairvoyance. What is more, we discover a higher, spiritual world behind all that lives, the world of the Second Hierarchy. It is important to be clear about this, for it sounds very dry and theoretical if we merely list the spirits that belong to the different hierarchies. Living ideas of what is alive and active behind the world perceived through the senses will only be gained if we know the road to be taken in the clairvoyant state of consciousness.

Yesterday we sought to characterize the spirits of the Third Hierarchy; today let us try and do the same for the Second Hierarchy, again taking our start from the human being. We said yesterday that instead of human sensory perception, the spirits of the Third Hierarchy have the revelation of their own essential nature, and in place of human inwardness something we may call 'being filled with the spirit'. Entering into the spirits of the Second Hierarchy we find that sensory perception has not merely become a revelation of their own essential nature, but that this revelation is retained as an independent principle, quite distinct from the spirits themselves. We can get an idea of this if we think of a snail secreting its shell. The shell, we can imagine, consists of a substance which had previously been part of the snail's body. Secreting its shell the snail not only reveals its essential nature to the outside world but has also secreted something which then has separate existence. This is how it is with the essential nature, the selfhood, of the spirits in the Second Hierarchy. They not only reveal their self, as the spirits of the Third Hierarchy do, but secrete it so that it becomes a separate entity.

We will be able to see this more clearly if we visualize a spirit from the Third Hierarchy on the one hand, and a spirit from the Second Hierarchy on the other. Turning the inner eye to a spirit from the Third Hierarchy we recognize it because it reveals its selfhood, its inwardness, to the outside world and in doing so gains perception; if its inner perception, its inner life, changes, the revelation also changes. The revelation of a spirit from the Third Hierarchy is therefore always changing. This is different when we turn the occult eye to a spirit from the Second Hierarchy. This also develops ideas, has inner experiences, but it secretes this out like a shell or a skin that has its own essential nature. And when the spirit develops a different kind of inwardness, developing new ideas and thus revealing itself in a new way, the old revelation of its essential nature continues to exist; it does not vanish, as it does with a spirit of the Third Hierarchy. With the Second Hierarchy, therefore, the creation of a kind of shell or skin may be said to take the place of revelation. It is thus the character of a spirit from the Second Hierarchy to create an image of itself, to make itself objective in a kind of image.

If we ask ourselves what takes the place of 'being filled with the spirit' in the Second Hierarchy, the occult eye perceives that each time a spirit secretes such an image or shell that bears the mark of its essential nature, life stirs within this spirit. The excitation of life always follows such self-creation.

For the Third Hierarchy we must therefore distinguish between the outer revelation and being inwardly filled with spirit, and for the Second Hierarchy between an outer aspect that is 'creating an image of the self, making it objective' and an inner aspect where life is stirring, as if a fluid were in continuous gentle motion within itself but froze on the outside, thus creating its own image. This is approximately what the occult eye sees as the outer and inner aspect of the spirits from the Second Hierarchy. To the occult eye, the way the spirits of the Third Hierarchy are filled with the spirit appears as a kind of spiritual light perceived as an image, but this gentle flow of life, this stirring of life, which is connected with external secretion, appears to occult perception rather like sounds heard in the spirit, music of the spheres. It is like sound heard in the spirit, not light of the spirit as in the case of the Third Hierarchy.

The spirits of the Second Hierarchy can be differentiated into categories, like those of the Third Hierarchy. It is, however, more difficult to perceive the differences, because things keep getting harder as we progress to the higher hierarchies. Initially we have to develop an idea of everything in the world around us that has form. As I said, at the second stage of clairvoyance this concerns only living entities and not the entities that appear lifeless to us. Those living entities have form, however. Plants have their forms, as do animals and human beings. If the clairvoyant eye, with all the properties we have described today, turns to everything to be found in the world of nature around us, leaving aside everything except form and shape, considering the rich variety of form seen in the plant world, the animal world and in human beings, the clairvoyant eye perceives the Spirits of Form who are members of the Second Hierarchy, the Exusiai.

We can also perceive something other than form in the entities that live around us. We know that all living things change shape, in some respects, as they grow. This change in shape, metamorphosis of form, is most apparent in the plant world. Turning the clairvoyant eye of the second stage rather than ordinary attention to the growing plant world, we see how a plant gradually evolves its specific shape in progressing from root to leaf shape, flower and fruit. We observe the growing animal, the growing human being—in short, we are not merely observing a shape that presents itself for the moment, but the growth and development of life forms. If we are stimulated by the changes in shape, by the living metamorphosis we see, the clairvoyant eye of the second stage perceives the category of the Spirits of Movement, the Dynamis.

It is more difficult to observe the third category of spirits in the Second Hierarchy. Now we need to observe not the shape, nor the movement, the changes in shape, but what comes to expression in form and shape. We can characterize how people can train themselves to make such observation. It is not a question of training the ordinary conscious mind by the method which I am describing, but of training a mind that has already been developed in clairvoyance. The observations can be made in our ordinary state of mind, but this will at most give a vague notion, a guess at what lies behind the facial expression and gestures of a person. When a mind trained to the second stage of clairvoyance takes in the physiognomy, gestures and expressions of a person, this stimulates ideas that will gradually train it to observe the spirits of the third category in the Second Hierarchy. This will not happen—please take note—if we do no more than merely observe the gestures, facial expressions and physiognomy of a person. Little will be achieved in this way.

It will be best to move on to plants for one's occult training. The animals can be left out; it is not particularly important to train oneself by observation of animals. What is important is that—having trained oneself a little in clairvoyance to take the facial expressions, physiognomy and gestures of a person as gateways to living experience of their inner soul life—one turns to the plant world and continues one's training there. Someone with training in clairvoyance will have some strange experiences, being able to get a profound feeling for the difference between a leaf that comes to a point (a) and a leaf with this shape (b); between a flower growing upwards in this way (c) and one that opens up to the outside more or less like this

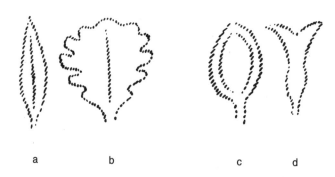

a   b   c   d

(d). Whole worlds of different inner experiences open up when the second-stage clairvoyant eye is turned to a lily or a tulip; when one takes in the panicle of an oat or a head of wheat or barley. All this comes alive and speaks to us as much as the physiognomy of a person does. And when we feel that a flower opening up to the outside has something of the nature of a hand that opens up to the outside palm down, back up, and then find a flower where the petals come together at the top like the movement when two hands are put together in prayer—if we feel the gestures and physiognomy of the plant world, and sense a kind of physiognomy in the colour of a flower, the occult inner eye comes alive, as do occult perception and occult understanding, and we recognize a third category of spirits in the Second Hierarchy whom we call the Spirits of Wisdom.

The name serves as an analogy, for if we observe the mien, physiognomy and gestures of a person, we see his spiritual principle, filled with wisdom, sprout forth, presenting itself. We can feel how spirits from the Second Hierarchy are present everywhere in the world of nature, coming to expression in the total gesture, the total mien, of nature. Wisdom filled with life flows and moves through all life forms, all realms of nature, and it is far from general but differentiated into a multitude of spiritual entities, the multitude of the Spirits of Wisdom. It is as though occult awareness rises to perception of those spirits, the highest level we can reach in this way.

But just as the spirits of the Third Hierarchy—Angels, Archangels and Spirits of the Times—had offspring who split off from them, so the spirits of this Second Hierarchy also have offspring. In the course of time spirits split off from those of the Second Hierarchy—in a way similar to that described yesterday for the Third Hierarchy—and become a lower category that is sent down into the realms of nature, like the nature spirits who are the offspring of the Third Hierarchy, who may be said to be builders and foremen on a smaller scale in the realms of nature.

The spirits who have split off from the Second Hierarchy to enter into the realms of nature are called the 'group souls' of plants and animals in occult terminology. Directed to the members of the plant and animal kingdoms, therefore, the second-stage occult eye finds entities that are the spirits not of individuals, as in the case of humans, but of groups of animals and plants, all of them given form and ensouled by a common spiritual entity. Let us say we find the form of the lions, the form of the tigers, and other forms ensouled by a common soul nature. These are the group souls, spiritual entities split off from the Second Hierarchy just as the nature spirits are the offspring of the Third Hierarchy.

And so we enter into the higher worlds from below, discovering that within the elements that are important to all members of the plant, animal and human worlds—the solid, fluid and gaseous elements—live the nature spirits who are the offspring of the Third Hierarchy. Progressing from the elements of earth, water and air to all that lives in the realms of nature with the help of these elements, we discover spirits that enter into the life-forms of those realms, giving them life; these are the group souls, which have split off from the spirits of the Second Hierarchy.

You can see, therefore, that the second category of entities known as group souls can indeed be perceived with the occult eye. Occult development must have reached the stage where the individual is able to reach out with his ether body as with tentacles before it is possible to know the spirits of the Second Hierarchy and the group souls which exist in the different realms of nature. It is even harder to progress to the spirits of the First Hierarchy and their offspring in the realms of nature. We shall speak of them in the next lecture.

2. The First Hierarchy and the Divine Trinity

Helsingfors, 7 April 1912

Our study has taken us as far as the Second Hierarchy of spiritual entities and it was shown yesterday what a human soul has to do if it wishes to approach the nature of that hierarchy. It is even harder to find one's way to the spiritual entities who are members of the First Hierarchy, the highest we are able to reach at present. It has been stressed that special enhancement of the compassion and love we are able to feel even in ordinary life takes us on the occult path to the point where we are able to pour our own essential nature forth, as it were, and enter wholly into the spirits we wish to perceive. Note that the character of this is such that we extend our own nature like tentacles, pouring it into the other entity. But we continue to exist apart from those entities as far as our conscious awareness and our own inner life goes. This is characteristic of the second stage of clairvoyance of which we spoke. At this stage we know at any moment, even as we know ourselves to be one with other beings, that we ourselves also exist, apart from those other beings, as it were. This last remnant of egotistical feeling must cease if we are to reach the third stage of clairvoyance.

We have to give up all feeling that we exist somewhere in the world as separate entities. We have to reach a point where we not only pour ourselves out into other entities and stand apart with our own inner life, but really feel those other entities to be our self, going completely out of ourselves and losing the feeling that we are beside the others. If we thus enter into the others, we see ourselves as we were previously, as we are in ordinary life—as non-self. Let us say that having reached the third stage of clairvoyance we enter into an entity that belongs to one of the realms of nature. We then look at it not merely from where we are, nor do we merely enter into it as we do at the second stage of clairvoyance, but we know ourselves to be one with it and look back at ourselves from there. We now see ourselves as non-self. That is the difference between the third and the second stage. Having reached the third stage we are able to perceive the spirits of the Third and Second Hierarchies which have already been characterized and also other entities in our spiritual surroundings.

The spiritual entities we are then able to perceive are also in three categories. Entering into the essential nature of other people or of the higher animals and making this our training, we perceive predominantly the first category. It is not so much the perceptions we make in them that matter but the training process as such and the ability to perceive the spirits who are behind human beings and the higher animals, the Spirits of Will, or Thrones, as they are called in western esotericism. The only way to characterize them is to say that they are not flesh and blood, nor light, nor air, but consist of a substance we are only able to perceive in ourselves if we are aware of having a will. The lowest substance they consist of is will.

We can train ourselves further by entering in the same way into lower animals, turning the occult eye to their lives, or into plant life, not in the way described yesterday, observing gesture and mien, but becoming one with the plants and seeing ourselves from inside the plants. We then gain an inner experience for which no real comparison can be found in the world we normally live in. The nearest we come to understanding the qualities of the second category of spirits in the First Hierarchy is to take into heart and mind the achievements of serious, worthy individuals who spent many stages of their lives in gathering wisdom and, after many years rich in experience, have gathered so much wisdom that we are able to say to ourselves: when someone like this makes a judgement there is no personal will behind it but the accumulation of a long life, which has, in a way, made them impersonal. People who impress us as being impersonal in their wisdom, which appears as the flower and fruit of a mature life, can give us some kind of feeling for what we experience at the stage of clairvoyance we must now speak of.

The western esoteric term for these spirits is Cherubim. It is extremely difficult to characterize them, for the higher we go, the less are we able to use qualities known to us in everyday life to gain an idea of the greatness and sublime nature of these hierarchies. The Spirits of Will, who are the lowest category in the First Hierarchy, can still be characterized if we gain an idea of the nature of will, for will is the lowest substance they consist of. However, just considering the will as we experience it in humans or animals in ordinary life, and the feelings and thoughts of human beings, would not make it possible for us to characterize the spirits from the second category of the First Hierarchy. For this, we must go to special people who have amassed the overwhelming power of inner wisdom I have described. If we get a feeling for this wisdom, this is similar to the feeling an occultist has in the encounter with the Cherubim. Wisdom, gathered not in decades but through thousands, millions of years of world evolution, meets us in the sublime power of the spirits we call the Cherubim.

The spirits who form the highest category of the First Hierarchy, the Seraphim, are even more difficult to characterize. The only way to gain an idea of the impression the Seraphim make on the occult eye is perhaps the following. Let us continue the analogy we have just made. We observe someone who has gathered inner experience for decades and achieved overwhelming wisdom, and we imagine that, out of the highly impersonal wisdom of life he has gained, this individual fills his whole inner nature with a kind of inner fire. He then need not say anything but only stand in front of us, putting all the wisdom gathered in decades into the look of his eyes. His eyes can tell us of the pain and experiences gained through decades, and we can have the impression that these eyes speak as the world which we experience does.

We can imagine such a look, or imagine that such a wise person has reached a point where he not only speaks to us in words, but where the sound and the particular colouring given to his words reflect rich life experience, so that we hear a kind of undertone in what he says. It is as if he puts a certain How into his words, and in this How we perceive a world of life experience. This can give us a feeling similar to that known by an occultist who ascends to the Seraphim. It is like a look in the eyes that has matured through life, like decades of experience speaking to us, or a sentence spoken in such a way that we hear not only the thoughts expressed but hear that the sentence, the way it is spoken, has been achieved in pain and life experience; it is not theory but something fought for, suffered for, something that has gone through life's battles and victories to reach the heart. If we hear this undertone, we gain an idea of the impression a trained occultist has when he advances as high as the spirits who are called the Seraphim.

We have been able to characterize the spirits of the Third Hierarchy by saying that what in human beings is the capacity for sensory perception is in them revelation of self; what in human beings is inner life, the waking state of consciousness, is in them a state of being filled with spirit. We were able to characterize the spirits of the Second Hierarchy by saying that what in the spirits of the Third Hierarchy is revelation of self is in them self-realization, self-creation, making images of their own essential nature, and what in the Third Hierarchy is the state of being filled with spirit is in them the stirring of life, inner excitation of life in the process of secreting the self, making it objective. The self-creation of the Second Hierarchy can also be seen with the occult eye in the spirits of the First Hierarchy, but there is a difference. The objective material created by the spirits of the Second Hierarchy continues to exist for as long as these spirits remain connected with their creation. Note well—the spirits of the Second Hierarchy can create a kind of image of themselves, but this remains connected to them and cannot be separate from them. It remains with them, in a way.

The spirits of the First Hierarchy also objectify themselves, producing an image of their own essential nature and secreting it like a skin or shell that reflects their own nature. This separates from them and continues to exist in the world even if they separate from it. They do not carry their creation about with themselves; it continues to exist even if they leave it behind. This is a higher degree of objectivity than can be achieved by the Second Hierarchy. The spirits of the Second Hierarchy become active and have to stay with their works which would otherwise perish. Their works would be dead and disintegrate unless they remained in contact with them. They are independent and objective, but only for as long as the spirits remain connected with them. The spirits of the First Hierarchy are able to move away and leave their creations to continue an independent, objective existence.

We thus have the following: Third Hierarchy, revelation and being filled with spirit; Second Hierarchy, self-creation and stimulation of life; First Hierarchy, that is, Thrones, Cherubim and Seraphim, creative work giving independent existence to their works, not self creation but creation of a world. A separate, independent world is created by the spirits of the First Hierarchy, a world that reveals phenomena, facts, even when the spirits of the hierarchy are no longer connected with it.

We may now also enquire into the nature of the First Hierarchy's own life. This consists in the hierarchy gaining awareness of itself in the process of letting such objective, independent entities arise and separate from it. Their inner state of conscious awareness, inner experience, lies in the creation of entities and letting them become independent. We may say they see what they create, which becomes the world, and find themselves not by looking into themselves but by looking at the world and at their creatures. Their inner life is to create other essential natures and live in them. World creation is their outside life, creation of essential natures their inner life.

Reference has been made during these days to the offspring of the individual hierarchies, entities that split off from them. These are sent down into the realms of nature. We found the offspring of the Third Hierarchy to be the nature spirits, the offspring of the Second Hierarchy the group souls. The spirits of the First Hierarchy also have offspring who split off from them, and in a way I have already described them for you from a different point of view. This was right at the beginning of this course of lectures, when I spoke of the Spirits of the Periods (of Revolution) who organize and direct events happening in rhythmic sequence and repetition in the world of nature. The spirits of the First Hierarchy have offspring who organize the sequence of winter and summer, letting plants grow and wither away again. The rhythmic sequence that causes members of a particular animal species to have a specific life span within which they develop from birth to death, and everything else that shows recurrence in rhythmic sequence in the realms of nature—like night and day, the course of the year, the four seasons—is regulated by the Spirits of the Periods, the offspring of the First Hierarchy. We can characterize them the way we did a few days ago, or according to their origins, as we have done today.

Summing up, we may represent the essential nature of the three hierarchies as follows.

	First Hierarchy	
creating worlds	creating essential nature	Spirits of Periods
	Second Hierarchy	
creating self	stimulating life	group souls
	Third Hierarchy	
revelation	filled with spirit	nature spirits

To proceed with the task I have been set, we must consider the images which the trained occultist's eye is gradually able to perceive. Initially these are somewhat difficult. But let us put these images and ideas before our mind's eye today, for it will help us in the lectures that follow, when I am to present the whole life and essential nature of the realms of nature and of the heavenly bodies, to get used to seeing the way the spirits I have characterized relate to these. We should thus be able to get a clearer and clearer picture as we go on.

Speaking of the human being, we characterize him as he presents himself to the occult eye. You will find this in anthroposophical books such as my *Theosophy* and *Occult Science*. Looking at the human being from the occult point of view we say that the first and most external thing, perceptible to our eyes and our senses, is the physical body. This, then, we consider to be the first principle of the human being. The second principle is already seen as something beyond sensory perception, invisible when we are in our normal state of consciousness—the ether body. The third principle is the astral body. These three principles are essentially the enveloping part of the human being. There are also higher principles, and these have a soul quality. In ordinary life they are perceived as the inner life of a person, and just as we have a threefold enveloping principle so we also have a threefold soul—sentient soul, intellectual or mind soul, and spiritual soul. These aspects of human nature, from physical body to spiritual soul, are basically found in every human being today. The next higher aspect is the Spirit Self, or Manas, as some of you are used to calling it. The following aspect is one that will only be fully developed at a future time in human beings; we call it Life Spirit or Buddhi. And then there is the aspect we consider to be the true Spirit Man, Atma; it is the innermost human nature, but today still lies dormant within us and will only come alight as the true centre of our conscious mind at a later stage in Earth evolution. In a way the physical human body is a whole, the human ether body is a whole, and so are the other aspects of human nature. The human being in turn is an integral whole in which those different aspects combine and interact.

You have to realize, if we are to progress in our study, that there are spirits higher than the human being. These are so far above human nature that they do not have aspects which can be called physical body, etheric body, and so on. The aspects of these spirits are themselves spirits. The aspects of human beings are such that we cannot see them as beings but only as aspects that are an integral whole in themselves. We have to ascend to entities that do not have a physical body but instead have the Spirits of Form, as we have called them. If we say there is a higher category of entities that do not have a physical body, the way human beings do, but have another being as an aspect, we gain an idea of a spirit we have not yet characterized but now intend to characterize. To do so, we have to use the ideas we have evolved in the course of our studies.

As I said, it is difficult to arrive at these ideas, but analogy can help us to arrive at those we need in this case. Consider a beehive or ant heap and the individual bees. Understand that a beehive has a real spirit in its own right, existing as an entity, and that the individual bees are its parts just as your aspects are your individual parts. This gives you an analogy for entities that are even higher than those we have considered so far. They do not have a physical body, the way humans do, but something we must call an entity in itself, a Spirit of Form. We live in our physical body. The more sublime spirits live in such a way that Spirits of Form, or a Spirit of Form, if you will, is their lowest aspect. We humans also have an etheric body. Those sublime spirits have Spirits of Movement as their second aspect. Instead of a human astral body they have Spirits of Wisdom, instead of a sentient soul Thrones or Spirits of Will; instead of an intellectual soul they have Cherubim as their fifth aspect, and instead of a spiritual soul Seraphim as their sixth aspect. We look up to aspects we shall only gradually make our own in future times on Earth; they look up to something that goes altogether beyond the hierarchic system. We speak of our Manas, Buddhi, Atma, or Spirit Self, Life Spirit and Spirit Man. These sublime spirits look up from their seraphic aspect—as we look up from our spiritual soul—to a spirituality of primal origin. This is where these spirits have something analogous to what we call our inner life of the spirit.

It is extremely difficult to give an idea of the spiritual nature of the sublime spirits who are above the hierarchies. In the course of human evolution, different religions and philosophies have therefore cautiously avoided—and we may say they have shown a certain honesty in thus cautiously avoiding the issue—speaking of the spirits that are above the hierarchies in outspoken terms, using ideas relating to the world we perceive through the senses. In our own efforts to give an idea even of what lives in an occultist's soul when he perceives the Seraphim we had to use analogies that otherwise are found only in people with vast life experience. And everything we see as a pure expression of their life even in such people is not sufficient to characterize the Trinity that is above the Seraphim, as it were, as their highest principle, their Manas, Buddhi and Atma.

Sadly, the tentative ideas developed by human minds in the course of evolution as to what exists in these realms of spirit have been the subject of much dispute. We may say 'sadly' because it would be much more appropriate for human minds not to attempt characterization of spiritual principles of such a sublime nature using the rough and ready ideas developed by all kinds of analogy and comparison with ordinary life. It would be much more appropriate if people developed a spirit of profound veneration, wanting to learn more and more of what exists up in those heights. Religious teachers and philosophers have tried to give approximate ideas by using terms that have a wide range of meaning and which may be said to be special in so far as they go beyond the life of the individual even in the world we perceive through the senses. Such terms do not even approximately characterize the sublime spirits in question, but they may give an idea of something that cannot be put in words but needs to be shrouded in sacred mystery.

For it would be wrong to seek direct access to these things with profane concepts gained from the outside world. In successive religions and philosophies attempts were therefore made to characterize these things in a mysterious way, finding names to characterize them by considering elements that go far beyond human nature and hold mystery even in the world of nature.

The ancient Egyptians used the concepts 'child' or 'son', 'mother' and 'father', something beyond the individual. In Christianity, attempts were made to give this trinity a name by using the sequence 'Holy Spirit', 'Son' and 'Father'. If we thus look up to a spirit the highest content of which appears to be disappearing into a mystery of the spirit, and try to suggest it by calling it 'Holy Spirit', 'Son' and 'Father', we say the following as we look at this spiritual entity with the occult eye. Looking at the human being from outside, we consider the physical body to be the lowest aspect. Looking at such a spiritual entity in a way analogous to the way we look at the human being, we see the Spirit of Form, that is a spirit which assumes form, a formed, shaped spirit. It should therefore be possible to look at the aspect of such an entity which is analogous to the physical body of man as something that has been given form.

The physical body of man as his lowest aspect is something that has been given shape and form. In truth this is illusory as it presents itself, for in it lives the Spirit of Form. Directing our eye to cosmic space and perceiving a planet—Mercury, Venus, Mars, Jupiter—we perceive the outer form of the Spirit of Form, something which is part of the entity we are considering just as the physical body is part of a human being. When we have a human being before us, the form expresses the higher aspects—ether body, astral body, sentient soul, and so on—that live in this human being. When we see a planet, its form expresses the form of the Spirits of Form. Behind the human form, behind the physical body, are etheric body, astral body, sentient soul and so on. Behind the planet and belonging to it are the Spirits of Movement, of Wisdom, of Will, Seraphim, Cherubim and so on. To consider the full nature of a planet in terms of the science of the spirit we must therefore say that in cosmic space the planet shines out to us in the physical form it has been given by the Spirits of Form. And just as man hides his higher aspects behind his physical appearance, so does the planet hide the spirits of the higher hierarchies that are active in and around it. We get the right image of a planet such as Mars or Mercury if we first of all visualize its physical form and then in our mind's eye see it surrounded and penetrated by a spiritual atmosphere that reaches out to infinity. This has its physical form, the creation of the Spirits of Form, in the physical planet, with the spirits of the other hierarchies all around it. We only have the complete planet if we see the physical as a central core, with enveloping spiritual principles that are the spirits of the hierarchies.

To give some indication of the direction in which this approach is going, let me say the following, for the moment merely reporting what occult research has shown.

As already said, if we consider the physical form of a planet this is the creation of the Spirits of Form. Our own human form on Earth is also a creation of the Spirits of Form. You know that our Earth is not at rest but always subject to inner change and mobility. You will remember the description from the Akashic Record according to which the outward appearance of the Earth is different today from what it was during the evolutionary period we call the Atlantean age, for instance. In those ancient Atlantean days the area now covered by the Atlantic Ocean was a mighty continent, whereas continents were barely beginning to evolve where Europe, Asia and Africa are today. The mass or substance of the Earth has thus shifted, due to inner mobility. The planet shows continuous inner mobility. Just think, for example, that Heligoland as we know it today is only a small part of an island which extended far out to sea in the ninth and tenth centuries. The periods in which repositioning, inner changes in the face of the Earth take place are relatively long, but we do not have to go into great detail to be able to say that the planet shows continuous inner mobility. What is more, if we count not only the solid earth as part of the planet but also water and air, we know from everyday experience that the planet has inner movement. As clouds form, rain falls, in all weather phenomena, with water rising and falling, planetary substance shows inner mobility. This is the life of the planet. Within this life of the planet the spirits we call the Spirits of Movement are active, just as the ether body is active in the life of an individual human being.

We are thus able to say that the outer form of the planet is created by the Spirits of Form. Inner liveliness is regulated by entities we call the Spirits of Movement.

To the occultist, such a planet is a genuine entity, an entity that regulates the processes which occur within it by means of thoughts. A planet thus not only has the internal liveliness we have described but the planet as a whole also has consciousness, for it is indeed an entity. This conscious awareness, which corresponds to human conscious awareness in so far as the lower form of consciousness, the subconscious, is within the astral body, is regulated for the planet by the Spirits of Wisdom. We are thus able to say that the lowest level of the planet's consciousness is regulated by the Spirits of Wisdom. With this characterization we are still inside the planet. We look up to the planet and say to ourselves: it has a certain form, which is in accord with the Spirits of Form; it has an inner mobility, which is in accord with the Spirits of Movement; all this is filled with consciousness, which is in accord with the Spirits of Wisdom. But let us take this further. The planet moves through space, it has an inner impulse that takes it through space just as humans have an inner will impulse that makes them take steps, moving in space. The principle which takes the planet through space, regulating its movement in space, making it move around a fixed star, for instance, is in accord with the Spirits of Will. They give the planet the impulse to move through space. The movement of the planet in space is thus in accord with the Spirits of Will or Thrones. If these were only to give the impulse of motion, every planet would go its own way in the universe. That is not the case, however, for every planet moves in harmony with the whole system. Its movement is regulated not only to make it move but to bring order into the whole planetary system. Order is created when a group of people who have each been going in different directions begin to follow a common goal. This is the way in which planetary movements are regulated, so that they are harmonized. It is the Cherubim who attune the movements of one planet with those of another, each taking account of the other. The Cherubim regulate the concerted movements of the planetary system. Every planetary system with its fixed star, which may be said to be the leader under the guidance of the Cherubim, also relates to other planetary systems that belong to different fixed stars. They agree with one another concerning their locations in space relative to the neighbouring systems, just as human beings come to mutual agreements and discuss how to do things together. Human beings establish a social system by means of mutual agreement, and this also applies to planetary systems. Mutual agreement exists between one fixed star and another. This alone creates the cosmos. The Seraphim regulate the way planetary systems 'speak' to each other in cosmic space in order to become a cosmos.

This has taken us through everything we find in human beings up to the level of the spiritual soul. Beyond this we come to the higher life of the spirit which alone gives meaning to the whole system up to the spiritual soul. Going beyond the Seraphim, we come to the principle we have today tried to characterize at least in part as the highest trinity. We come to the divine, threefold divine life that prevails throughout the universe and creates enveloping forms for itself in the individual planetary systems. The Spirit Self, Life Spirit and Spirit Man—Manas, Buddhi and Atma—that live in human beings

create enveloping forms for themselves in spiritual, intellectual and sentient soul, astral, etheric and physical bodies. In
the same way the fixed stars of the planetary systems move
through space as the bodies of divine spirits. Looking at life in
the world of the stars we behold the bodies of the gods and
ultimately of the divine principle as such.

3. Future Jupiter Existence

Dornach, 3 January 1915

If you recall the talks we had in connection with the evolution of the Earth through the Saturn, Sun and Moon periods, you will remember that at each of these evolutionary stages spirits of one particular level from among what we would now call the higher hierarchies attained their own human level. We know that during the Old Saturn period the Spirits of Personality, Prime Origins or Archai reached their human level, during the Old Sun period the Archangels, during the Old Moon period the Angels and during the Earth period, mankind.

You will also have seen from our talks on evolution that each level of spirits that subsequently reached a certain stage of development first underwent preparation for this. We know that the human being was being prepared throughout the Saturn, Sun and Moon periods, and that the completed physical human body as we know it today has been evolving since the Saturn period, the ether body since the Sun period, the astral body since the Moon period, while the ego was only added during the Earth period.

You may be anxious to know whether in our present period of evolution other entities are being prepared to attain their human level in the Jupiter period. You know that during the Saturn, Sun and Moon periods—you can look it up in my book *Occult Science*[14]—the spirits of the higher hierarchies took part in the preparation of humanity. A description is given of how the Angels, Archangels and Archai were involved in the development of human beings. An obvious question is whether human beings, during their Earth existence, are perhaps involved in preparing the entities who will reach their human level during the Jupiter period.

This question is certainly important to every sensitive person—sensitive in the sense of having been inspired by the science of the spirit in the way I have described. Might it be the case that human behaviour in general during the course of Earth evolution could either help, or fail to help, the entities who may attain their human level in the Jupiter period? We could say, 'What can be worse than behaving in such a way during Earth evolution as to make it impossible for proper Jupiter spirits to arise through our actions?'

If we want to talk about these things we must of course take it for granted that there is a degree of good will towards this knowledge, for these are truly important secrets of initiation, the kind of initiation secrets that modern scientists detest as a matter of course. One certainly has to be sensitive in preparing to look at the attitude modern scientists are bound to have to the real truths of life.

In the previous lectures I have tried to say a little about the way modern science necessarily relates to life. It has no direct access to the secrets of life and cannot even want this. But scientists should not even pretend to want to reach these secrets of life. It may be a good thing to make hard-boiled eggs for people who like their eggs hard-boiled, and hard-boiled eggs are useful for those who like them. But if we were to go and say that we are taking the eggs away from the hens to hard-boil them, and then put them back for the hens to hatch, we would be doing something absurd. As far as the cosmos is concerned we would be doing exactly the same thing if we were to set out to solve its secrets by means of modern science. This is exactly the same attitude as wanting to hatch hard-boiled eggs that never will hatch.

Let me use an analogy to show you just how misleading this science is that is bound up with the whole way of modern thinking, particularly when it comes to the real riddles of life. Those wanting to hold forth about whether science is helpful or harmful will usually start off by asking: 'Is science right about this or that?' If they can prove that it is right in one instance or another, they will have absolute confidence in it as a matter of course.

Attaching so much importance to the question of whether what science says is right or not is the very attitude we have to get away from. We must reach the point of seeing that this is not the main thing when it comes to solving the riddles of life. If you see a horse-drawn cart with a man in it, you will be quite right in saying that the horses are pulling this person in the cart and drawing him along behind them. This is correct, of course; and anyone who wanted to say that the horses were not drawing the cart with the man sitting in it, would obviously be wrong. But it is also true that the man sitting in the cart is guiding the horses, controlling the direction in which they should go; and that is surely the more important aspect from the point of view of the destination. Modern science can be said to be like someone who denies that the man in the cart is guiding the horses and who will only admit that the horses are drawing the man in the cart.

If you think this analogy through, you will get the right idea about the relation of modern science to modern research into truth. I have to say these things over and over again, because those who base themselves on our view of the world must become increasingly capable of defending and protecting the point of view of spiritual science against attacks from people who have the modern world outlook. But you will be able to do this only if you have a clear idea as to the relation of modern external science to genuine research into truth. You must always approach questions of spiritual science with a quite specific attitude and a specific nuance of feeling, otherwise you will not cope properly with them.

Our question concerning the entities who will reach the human level on Jupiter is indeed connected with the deepest questions of human evolution on Earth. Something in our Earth evolution has always been a philosophical problem, namely the relation between moral behaviour and natural existence. As earthly beings we have to decide to what extent we are ruled by our instincts and are forced to obey and satisfy them, to what extent we are at the mercy of our instincts and their satisfaction because the laws of nature simply insist on their being satisfied. That is one side of human nature. In this respect we say: 'We do these things because we have to. We must eat and we must sleep.'

But there is another sphere of human conduct on this Earth, a sphere in which we cannot say 'must', for it would lose its whole significance if we were to say 'must' here. This is the wide sphere of 'shall', a sphere where we feel that we have to follow a purely spiritual impulse rather than our instincts and everything arising out of ourselves on the natural level. 'You shall' never speaks to us out of our instincts but directs us in a purely spiritual way. 'You shall' comprises the sphere of our moral obligations.

Some philosophers cannot distinguish between what is implied by 'you shall' as opposed to 'you must'. Our present age is almost bogged down in materialism, especially where moral life is concerned—and it will get more and more bogged down—and people would therefore like to turn all 'you shalls' into 'you musts'. We are heading for times when, in this respect, turning 'you shall' into 'you must' will be acclaimed with a certain amount of arrogance, and actually called psychology. Terrible prospects open up if we look at what has begun to develop, for example in the field of criminal psychology. The tendency is not to ask whether someone has overstepped a 'you shall', but to try and prove that the person was driven to some destructive act out of a necessity of inherent nature. Strange attempts are on the increase to define crime merely as a particular case of illness. All this arises from a certain materialistic lack of clarity in our times regarding the distinction between 'you shall' and 'you must'.

What does this 'you shall', or in other words the categorical imperative, actually signify within the whole context of human existence? We know that someone who obeys the 'you shall' carries out a moral action. Someone who does not obey the 'you shall' commits an immoral action. This is of course merely an everyday truth. But let us now attempt to look at 'moral' and 'immoral' not only with regard to the external maya of the physical plane but with regard to the truth and what actually exists behind physical maya. Here the moral, the ethical element corresponding to the 'you shall' appears to initiation science as something that hits you in the eye, spiritually, to put it rather crudely. If you look at a person—these truths which the materialistic outlook detests have to be told some time—if you look at someone in certain temperature and weather conditions—you see this even better in horses, but we are not speaking about horses now—you will see him breathing out, and the breath becoming visible as vapour in the air. Obviously as far as materialistic science is concerned this breath disperses and dissolves and has no further significance. But it has significance for someone who follows up the phenomena of life through initiation science, for he sees in the patterns of the breath the exact traces of the moral or immoral conduct of the person. A person's moral or immoral behaviour can be seen in the vaporous breath, and the breath of a person who is morally inclined is quite different from the breath of a person who is inclined to immorality. Certain more subtle qualities can only be detected in the more subtle parts of the etheric and astral aura. But the human being's moral and immoral tendencies in the ordinary sense of the word are actually visible in the etheric and astral content of the vaporous breath. The physical part of it dissolves. But what is incorporated in it does not dissolve; for it contains a demonic being which, in the case of breath containing water vapour, has a physical, an etheric and an astral part, only the physical is not earthy, just watery. Highly differentiated forms can be seen in this breath.

When actions are done out of love something quite different manifests compared with actions done out of enthusiasm, a creative urge or the urge for perfection. But in every case the form in the breath reminds one of entities who do not at all exist on Earth today. They are a preparation for the ones who will reach their human stage on Jupiter. Their forms are very changeable and will pass through further changes in the future, for these are the first advance shadowy images of the entities who will reach the human level on Jupiter.

In a sense we ourselves owe our existence to the exhalation of the Angels on the Old Moon; and it is one of the deeply moving experiences of spiritual life to know that Jupiter human beings of the future will evolve out of what we breathe out today. If we approach the Bible with such knowledge in mind, and read the opening words, we can say to ourselves, 'Now we begin to understand what is meant when it says that breaths were exhaled by the Elohim and that the Elohim formed earthly man by breathing into him.'

I will confess that I would never have understood the part about the Elohim breathing the living being of man into his mouth and nostrils if I had not known beforehand that the breath of earthly human beings also contains the first germinal beginnings of the entities who will become human on Jupiter. But Jupiter human beings can only arise from the kind of breath that owes its existence to actions that obey the 'you shall', and which are therefore moral actions.

Thus we see how with our earthly morality we play a creative part in the whole cosmic order. Our earthly morality is indeed a creative power, and we can see that spiritual science gives us a strong impulse for moral action by telling us that we are working against the creation of Jupiter human beings if we do not act in a moral way on Earth. This gives morality, the expression of 'you shall', a very real value, an existential value. Our human conduct is intensely determined by what we are able to learn through the science of the spirit, especially as we truly perceive secrets connected with the cosmos.

I have referred to similar things in the past, also saying at various times that speech symbolizes man's own future creativity. I do not wish to dwell on this today though, but just wanted to show you the significance of moral behaviour for the cosmos as a whole.

You could now ask: 'What about immoral behaviour?' Immoral behaviour, too, comes to expression in the inner configuration of the breath. But immoral behaviour imprints a demonic form in it. Demons are born through man's immoral conduct. Let us look at the difference between the demons that arise through immoral behaviour and the spiritual entities—spiritual in so far as they only achieve a watery existence on Earth—the spiritual forms that are created by moral actions.

The entities which achieve transient watery existence and arise from moral conduct are the kind who have an astral, an etheric and finally a physical body condensed to the level of wateriness, just as, in the Old Moon period, we had an etheric, an astral and a physical body, and this physical body was also only condensed to a watery level. This is more or less, though not quite, what we were like during the Old Moon period. The configuration arising out of moral actions and possessing a physical body, ether body and astral body has a predisposition to receive an I or ego, just as in the Old Moon period our physical, etheric and astral bodies were predisposed to receive an ego. They are predisposed to receive an ego, and entities of this kind are qualified to undergo a regular progressive evolution in the cosmos.

The demons created out of immoral actions also have an astral body, an ether body and a physical body, at the watery level, of course, but they do not have the basis for developing an ego. They are born headless, as it were. They do not take up the basis for regular evolution to Jupiter existence but reject it. By doing so they condemn themselves to a fate of dropping out of evolution and adding to the hordes of luciferic beings, falling into their power. Unable to progress in a regular way they have to become parasites. This is what happens to all the spirits who reject normal evolution; they have to attach themselves to others in order to progress. Spirits who arise through immoral actions have a particular tendency to be parasites in human evolution on Earth under Lucifer's leadership, and to seize hold of the evolution of human beings before these make their physical entry into the world. They attack human beings during the embryonic stage and share their existence between conception and birth. Some of these spirits, if they are strong enough, can continue to accompany the human being after birth, creating the phenomena seen in children who are possessed.

The criminal demons attached as parasites to unborn children cause deterioration in the succession of the generations; this eats into human beings, making them less good than they would be if these demons did not exist. There are various reasons for the decline of families, tribes, peoples and nations, but one of them is the existence of these criminal demon parasites during the period mentioned.

These things play an important part in Earth evolution as a whole, and we are here touching on deep secrets of human existence. People often acquire certain prejudices and points of view even before they are born because of this. They are then tormented by doubts and uncertainties in life, and all kinds of other things, because of these demonic parasites.

These spirits cannot do very much once human beings develop their ego, but they prey on them all the more before they are born or in their earliest years. Thus we see that evil actions also have a significant effect in the cosmos and work creatively, but their creativity tends in the direction of the Old Moon existence. For in the embryonic period, when these demonic beings can prey on them, human beings basically go through the heritage of the Old Moon period, which shows itself in all kinds of subconscious, instinctive behaviour. Something stemming from older and better times has made material science preserve an instinct, so that the human embryonic period is calculated in 10 lunar rather than ordinary months. Scientists thus speak of 10 lunar months, and they also know other things concerning the connection of embryonic development with the phases of the moon.

So we see two trends in our Earth evolution. Good deeds contain the impulse to work creatively on Earth in preparation for Jupiter, so that man's successor on the human level can come into being. Evil deeds have brought into our evolution the tendency to take the Earth back again to the Old Moon period and make it dependent on everything to do with subconscious impulses. If you think about it you will find a great number of things that are connected with these subconscious impulses; in fact, there are far more of these subconscious impulses in materialistic humanity of modern times than there were in bygone ages when people were less materialistic.

I believe that the kind of things I have been telling you about again today will make you aware of the deep impression spiritual science can make on your outlook on life, and that it will definitely give you not only theoretical knowledge but will be capable of giving human life a new direction. A time will come when life will become quite chaotic if people do not use the chance of giving it a new direction out of spiritual science. People must get beyond knowledge that is restricted to physical circumstances. Our materialistic age does not want knowledge of any other sort than the kind that is restricted to the physical body. But people must lift their knowledge out of this physical body. The first exercises in *Knowledge of the Higher Worlds*[16] will gradually—though 'gradually' will be quite a long time—turn into something we do naturally, something we will feel to be second nature. Particularly what we call mental concentration will come naturally to people.

People will more and more feel the need to concentrate fully in their thoughts, to focus their whole soul activity on clearly defined thoughts, keeping them firmly in mind. While they would otherwise let their senses roam from one thing or fact to another, they will more and more often direct their thought life to specific things of their own choosing; even if only for a short time, they will concentrate on a particular thought, so as to focus the whole of their inner life on this thought. They will then discover something which many of you know very well. Everyone makes a particular discovery when concentrating. If we put a thought at the centre of our conscious mind and focus the whole of our inner life on it, we find the thought gets stronger and stronger. It certainly does. But there comes a point when it does not get stronger but weaker and fades away. This is an experience many of you will have had. The thought has to fade away; it has, as it were, to die away inwardly. For the kind of thoughts we have the way we generally think arise through the instrument of the physical body, and we concentrate the kind of thinking we do by means of the instrument of the physical body until the moment comes when the thought dies; at this moment we slip out of the physical body.

We would altogether enter into the unconscious if we did not also attempt to do something else which allows us to maintain consciousness when we have slipped out of the physical body. What we have to do to maintain consciousness when we are outside is to lead a calm and composed life, accepting the things of the world with composure. We can do even more than this. We can take seriously a theory we know very well, namely, the concept of karma. What do I mean?

People are not at all inclined at first to take the idea of karma really seriously. If they have even a small mishap that proves painful or anything at all happens to them, they will sometimes get furious or at any rate feel antipathy towards it. We meet what we call our destiny with sympathy or antipathy. In ordinary life this has to be so; it is essential that we feel sympathy towards some destiny events and antipathy towards others. To us, destiny is something that comes to meet us from outside.

If we take the idea of karma seriously, we must fully recognize our ego in our destiny and realize we ourselves are active in what happens to us through destiny; that we are the actual agents. When someone offends us it is certainly difficult to believe that we ourselves are inside the offender. For it may be necessary in physical life to punish the offence. But we must always keep a private corner within us where we admit to ourselves: 'Even when someone offends me it is me offending myself; when someone hits me it is me hitting myself, when unpleasant strokes of destiny hit me, I am dealing these blows myself.' We forget that we are not only within our skin but also in our destiny; we forget we are within all the 'chance' events in our destiny.

It is very difficult genuinely to acquire the attitude that our own ego brings us our destiny. But it is true that with our own ego we bring ourselves our destiny, and we get the impulses for this in the life between death and a new birth according to our earlier incarnations, so that we can bring ourselves our destiny. We must seek to unite with our destiny and, instead of warding off hard blows of fate with antipathy, tell ourselves more and more often: 'Through having this blow of destiny, that is, through bringing this stroke of destiny on myself, I am making myself stronger, more vigorous and robust.'

It is more difficult to unite with your destiny than to resist it, but what we lose when the thought dies in us can only be regained by drawing into ourselves, like this, what is outside us. We cannot stay in what is within our skin if the thought fades when we concentrate on it, but it will take us out of ourselves if we have taken hold of our destiny, our karma, in the true sense. We thus awaken ourselves again. The thought dies, but we carry with us the identification we have grasped between our ego and our destiny, and this carries us about in the world outside.

Composure with respect to our destiny, sincere acceptance of destiny, is what gives us existence when we are outside our body. Obviously this does not need to affect our life on the physical plane. We cannot always do it. But the attitude we have to acquire in the privacy of our soul must be there for the moments when we really want to be able to live consciously outside our body.

Two maxims can be our guiding principles and can mean a very great deal to us. The first of these to impress upon our minds is:

Seek to let thought die away in the universe.

For thought becomes a living force outside us only when it dies away in the universe. Yet we cannot unite ourselves with this living force unless we work at the content of the second maxim:

Seek to let destiny be resurrected in the 'I'.

If I achieve this, I unite the I that has been reborn in the thought with the I resurrected outside me.

Much in human nature makes it difficult, however, to progress in accord with these maxims. It is particularly hard to look at the relationship between inner and outer in the right way. The more we can learn morally from spiritual science in this connection, the better. We can learn what is moral from it in so far as certain ethical concepts acquire life and blood for the first time through what spiritual science can bring to them.

For instance, some people are always complaining about others and the awful things they do to them. They even go so far as to say that other people are persecuting them. Everything of this kind is always connected with the other pole of human nature; you only have to observe life in the right way, which means according to spiritual science as properly understood. Of course there is good reason to complain about unkindness, but in spite of this you will always find, if you go through life with vision that has been somewhat clarified by spiritual science, that most of these complaints come from egotists, and that the suspicion that everyone wants to be nasty to them arises most often in egotistical natures, whereas those with a loving disposition will not readily suspect persecution, nor that people are trying to harm them in all kinds of ways, and so on.

When it is put into words like this it is easy to agree with it in theory. In fact I am convinced that most people will admit to it theoretically, if they stop to think about it. But to live accordingly is what matters.

Now you may ask: 'How do we live accordingly?' And again the answer must be, 'You must truly join in the endeavour to enter as much as you can into the science of the spirit.' That is the point. That is why spiritual science is not given in compendia or short abstracts; we are trying to make spiritual science a living stream in which we can live and from which we can constantly draw stimulating impulses.

Notes

[GA = German edition of collected works of Rudolf Steiner]

1 Erigena, Johannes Scotus. Migne, Patrologia Latina 122, col. 912 c. Categories of nature.
2 Ibid. col. 982 BC.
3 Alanus ab Insulis. *Quoniam Homines*, ed. P. Glorieux. AHMA 1953; **28**: 137.
4 Thomas Aquinas: *Commentary* IV, 49.2.1.
5 Ibid.
6 Ibid.
7 Thomas Aquinas. *Summa Theologiae* 1, 88,1. Cf. Klünker WU. *Zur Anthropologie des Thomas von Aquin*, pp. 41 ff. Stuttgart 1990.
8 Ibid.
9 Ibid.
10 Thomas Aquinas. *Summa Theologiae* 1,88,1.
11 Dionysius the Areopagite. *On the Heavenly and Ecclesiastical Hierarchies*. This work appeared in the fifth century but was based on more ancient oral tradition.
12 Thomas Aquinas. *Summa Theologiae* 1.52.1. Cf. Klünker WU. *Selbsterkenntnis des Seele. Zur Anthropologie des Thomas von Aquin* pp 67 ff. Stuttgart 1990.
13 Thomas Aquinas. *Summa Theologiae* 1.52.2.
14 Steiner R. *Occult Science—An Outline* (GA 13). Tr. G. & M. Adams. London: Rudolf Steiner Press 1962.
15 Steiner R. *Spiritual Guidance of the Individual and Humanity* (GA 15). Tr. S. Desch. New York: Anthroposophic Press 1994.
16 Steiner R. *Knowledge of the Higher Worlds, How is it Achieved?* (GA 10). Tr. D. S. Osmond, C. Davy. London: Rudolf Steiner Press 1976.
17 The above paragraph does not entirely make sense; it seems that sentences or important parts of sentences have been omitted from the record. The meaning may be perceived by comparing

it with the statements made earlier in this lecture and in *Spiritual Guidance of the Individual and Humanity* (see note 15).

18 Steiner R. *Cosmic and Human Metamorphoses* (in GA 175), lecture of 13 February 1917. Tr. H. Collison. London: Anthroposophical Publishing Co. 1926.

19 Plutarch (*c.* 50–*c.* 120 AD), Greek historian and philosopher. The quoted passage has not been identified.

20 Theophrastus Bombastus von Hohenheim (1495–1541), Swiss alchemist, physician and scientist.

21 Steiner R. *Theosophy* (GA 9). Tr. M. Cotterel & A. P. Shepherd. London: Rudolf Steiner Press 1970.

22 Rudolf Steiner was speaking of the events of the First World War (1914–18).

23 See Steiner R. *Destinies of Individuals and of Nations* (GA 157). Tr. A. Meuss. London: Rudolf Steiner Press 1984.

24 Steiner R. 'Geist und Stoff, Leben und Tod' (GA 66). Lecture of 17 February 1917. Not available in English. Dornach: Rudolf Steiner Verlag.

25 Steiner R. 'Was wollte das Goetheanum und was soll die Anthroposophie?' Lecture given in Bern on 5 April 1923. Also a lecture with the same title given in Basel on 9 April 1923. Not available in English.

26 Especially in the following: Steiner R. *The Mission of Folk Souls* (GA 121). Tr. A. H. Parker. London: Rudolf Steiner Press 1970; *Cosmosophy* vol. 1 (GA 207). Tr. A. Wulsin, M. Kirkcaldy. New York: Anthroposophic Press 1985; *The Driving Force of Spiritual Powers in World History* (GA 222). Tr. D. Osmond, J. Collis. Toronto: Steiner Book Centre 1972.

27 Especially in Steiner R. *Manifestations of Karma* (GA 120). Tr. Rev. H. Herrmann-Davey. London: Rudolf Steiner Press 1995.

28 See note 25.

29 Steiner R. *On the Reality of Higher Worlds* (in GA 79). Lecture given in Oslo on 25 Nov 1921. Tr. D. Osmond. London: Anthroposophical Publishing Co. 1947; *Paths to Knowledge of Higher Worlds* (in GA 79). Lecture given in Oslo on 26 Nov 1921. Tr. not known. Toronto: Steiner Book Centre 1970.

30 Steiner R. *The Inner Nature of Man and the Life between Death and Rebirth*. Tr. D. Osmond, C. Davy. Rev. A. R. Meuss. Bristol: Rudolf Steiner Press 1994.

31 Steiner R. *The Soul's Awakening* in *The Four Mystery Plays* (GA 14). Tr. A. Bittleston. London: Rudolf Steiner Press 1982.

32 Steiner R. *The Mission of the Archangel Michael* (in GA 174a), lecture of 17 Feb 1918. Tr. L. Monges. New York: Anthroposophic Press 1961.

33 Steiner R. *Theosophy* (GA 9). Tr. M. Cotterell & A. P. Shepherd. London: Rudolf Steiner Press 1970. Also tr. C. E. Creeger. New York: Anthroposophic Press 1995.

34 Steiner R. *Cosmic Memory* (GA 11). Tr. K. E. Zimmer. New York: Harper and Row 1981.

35 Matthew 3:2 and 4:17; Mark 1:15.

36 Public lecture by Rudolf Steiner about spiritual research into 'questions of life and riddles of death' given in Stuttgart on 17 May 1913.

37 Janus was a Roman deity represented as having two faces, the god of beginnings.

38 Steiner R. *The Mission of Folk Souls* (GA 121). Tr. A. H. Parker. London: Rudolf Steiner Press 1970.

39 Steiner R. *Life Between Death and Rebirth* (GA 140). Tr. R. M. Querido. New York: Anthroposophic Press 1968.

40 Aristotle (384–322 BC), Greek philosopher, scientist and physician.

41 Aristotle. *Parva naturalia* ch. 3. See also Steiner R. *Goethe, the Scientist* (GA 1). Tr. O. D. Wannamaker. New York: Anthroposophic Press 1950.

42 St Albertus Magnus (*c.* 1200–80), Count of Bollstädt, *Doctor Universalis*, canonized in 1932. Thomas Aquinas was his student.

43 Helmholtz, Hermann von (1821–94), German physiologist and physicist. See Steiner R. *The Riddles of Philosophy* (GA 18). Tr. F. C. A. Kölln. New York: Anthroposophic Press 1973.

44 Svedberg, Theodor (1884–1971), Swedish chemist. 1926 Nobel prize. Inventor of ultracentrifuge for study of colloidal particles.

45 Basilius Valentinus, fifteenth-century alchemist.

46 Wagner. Figure in Goethe's *Faust*, Part One.

47 Steiner R. *The Spiritual Beings in the Heavenly Bodies and in the Kingdoms of Nature* (GA 136), lecture of 5 April 1912. Tr. unknown. Vancouver: Steiner Book Centre 1981.

Sources of the Lectures

'The Work of the Angel in our Astral Body'. Previously published as *The Work of the Angels in Man's Astral Body*, Rudolf Steiner Press, London, 1988. German = GA 182.

'Three Encounters between the Human Soul and Spirits of the Universe'. Previously published as *The Human Soul and the Universe*, Steiner Book Centre, North Vancouver, 1982. German = GA 175.

'The Shaping of Destiny in Sleep and in the Waking State'. Not previously translated. German = GA 224.

'The Human Being's Relationship to his Angel and to the Higher Hierarchies'. In: *Self-Consciousness, The Spiritual Human Being*, Garber Communications, New York, 1986. German = GA 209.

'Angels, Spirits of Nations, Spirits of the Times'. In: *The Mission of the Individual Folk Souls*, Rudolf Steiner Press, London, 1970. German = GA 121.

'The Michael Impulse and the Mystery of Golgotha'. In *The Festivals and their Meaning*, Rudolf Steiner Press, London, 1996. German = GA 152.

'Spiritual Entities Seen through the Ages'. In: *Rosicrucianism and Modern Initiation*, Rudolf Steiner Press, London, 1982. German = GA 233a.

'The Third and Second Hierarchies'. In: *Spiritual Beings in the Heavenly Bodies and in the Kingdoms of Nature*, Anthroposophic Press, New York, 1992. German = GA 136.

'The First Hierarchy and the Divine Trinity'. In: *Spiritual Beings in the Heavenly Bodies and in the Kingdoms of Nature*, Anthroposophic Press, New York, 1992. German = GA 136.

'Future Jupiter Existence'. In: *Art as seen in the Light of Mystery Wisdom*, Rudolf Steiner Press, London, 1996. German = GA 275.

Further Reading

Other works on the subject of the hierarchies by Rudolf Steiner

1 Books

Cosmic Memory (GA 11). Tr. K. E. Zimmer. New York: Harper and Row 1981.

Occult Science—An Outline (GA 13). Tr. G. & M. Adams. London: Rudolf Steiner Press 1962.

Spiritual Guidance of Man and Humanity (GA 15). Tr. H. Monges. New York: Anthroposophic Press 1983. Also available as *Spiritual Guidance of the Individual and Humanity* (GA 15). Tr. S. Desch. New York: Anthroposophic Press 1992.

Anthroposophical Leading Thoughts (GA 26) p. 99. Tr. G. & M. Adams. London: Rudolf Steiner Press 1973.

2 Lectures

The Influence of Spiritual Beings upon Man (GA 102). Tr. not known. New York: Anthroposophic Press 1961.

The Spiritual Hierarchies and their Reflection in the Physical World (GA 110). Tr. R. Querido. New York: Anthroposophic Press 1983.

The Mission of Folk Souls (GA 121). Tr. A. H. Parker. London: Rudolf Steiner Press 1970.

Genesis. Secrets of the Bible Story of Creation (GA 122). Tr. D. Lenn and O. Barfield. London: Rudolf Steiner Press 1982.

The Inner Realities of Evolution (in GA 132). Tr. not known. London: Rudolf Steiner Publishing Co. 1953.

The Spiritual Beings in the Heavenly Bodies and in the Kingdoms of Nature (GA 136). Tr. not known. Vancouver: Steiner Book Centre 1981.

Christ and the Spiritual World and The Search for the Holy Grail (GA 149). Tr. C. Davy and D. Osmond. London: Rudolf Steiner Press 1983.

Human and Cosmic Thought (GA 151). Tr. C. Davy. London: Rudolf Steiner Press 1967.

Cosmic and Human Metamorphoses (in GA 175). Tr. H. Collison. London: Anthroposophical Publishing Co. 1926.

The Fall of the Spirits of Darkness (GA 177), lecture given in Dornach on 14 October 1917. Tr. A. R. Meuss. Bristol: Rudolf Steiner Press 1993.

Individual Spirit Beings and the Undivided Foundations of the World (in GA 178). Tr. not known. Dornach: Philosophic-Anthroposophic Press 1930.

The Michael Revelation (in GA 194), lectures given in Dornach on 6 and 7 December 1919. Tr. M. A. Kaufmann. MS translations Z 415 at Rudolf Steiner House Library, London.

The Mission of Michael. The Revelation of the Intrinsic Secret of the Human Being (in GA 194). Tr. L. D. Monges. New York: Anthroposophic Press 1961.

The Mysteries of Light, of Space and of the Earth (in GA 194). Tr. F. E. Dawson. New York/London: Anthroposophic Press/Rudolf Steiner Publishing Co. 1945.

The Four Seasons and the Archangels (in GA 229), lecture of 5 October 1923. Tr. C. Davy and D. S. Osmond. London: Rudolf Steiner Press 1968.

Publisher's Note Regarding Rudolf Steiner's Lectures

The lectures contained in this volume have been translated from the German which is based on stenographic and other recorded texts that were in most cases never seen or revised by the lecturer. Hence, due to human errors in hearing and transcription, they may contain mistakes and faulty passages. Every effort has been made to ensure that this is not the case. Some of the lectures were given to audiences more familiar with anthroposophy; these are the so-called 'private' or 'members' lectures. Other lectures, like the written works, were intended for the general public. The difference between these, as Rudolf Steiner indicates in his *Autobiography*, is twofold. On the one hand, the members' lectures take for granted a background in and commitment to anthroposophy; in the public lectures this was not the case. At the same time, the members' lectures address the concerns and dilemmas of the members, while the public work speaks directly out of Steiner's own understanding of universal needs. Nevertheless, as Rudolf Steiner stresses: 'Nothing was ever said that was not solely the result of my direct experience of the growing content of anthroposophy. There was never any question of concessions to the prejudices and preferences of the members. Whoever reads these privately printed lectures can take them to represent anthroposophy in the fullest sense. Thus it was possible without hesitation—when the complaints in this direction became too persistent—to depart from the custom of circulating this material "for members only". But it must be borne in mind that faulty passages do occur in these reports not revised by myself.' Earlier in the same chapter, he states: 'Had I been able to correct them [the private lectures] the restriction *for members only* would have been unnecessary from the beginning.'

Other Selected Lectures by
Rudolf Steiner

SELF-TRANSFORMATION

At the heart of Rudolf Steiner's spiritual philosophy is the esoteric path of inner development that can lead to true self-transformation. In these lectures, Steiner shows how—by developing certain qualities such as clear thinking, inner tranquility and positivity, as well as through meditative exercises—it is possible to break out of the shadowy, brain-bound world of everyday consciousness. The first step on this path of transformation is the level of Imagination, where the spiritual world is seen in pictures. Steiner indicates how one can then attain to the levels of Inspiration, and finally to the highest stage of Intuition.

As a highly-trained clairvoyant, Rudolf Steiner speaks on this question from his own spiritual experience. In contrast to many of the New Age paths available today, however, his methods are based on the western tradition, the Rosicrucian path of initiation, as opposed to older Eastern teachings. This modern path is, he suggests, a metamorphosis of the Eastern paths, and is best suited to modern consciousness.

ISBN 1-855840-19-7; 256pp; £11.95

NATURE SPIRITS

In ancient times, when people had a natural spiritual vision, human beings communed with nature spirits. These spirits—which are also referred to as elemental beings—became known as fairies and gnomes, and are immortalised in myth, legend and stories for children.

It is Rudolf Steiner's contention, based on knowledge attained through his own highly-trained clairvoyance, that this aspect of traditional 'folk wisdom' is based on spiritual reality. In our time, he states, the instinctive understanding that humankind once had for these elemental beings must be transformed into a clear scientific knowledge. Without developing this new relationship to these beings, humanity will not be able to bridge the gulf that separates it from the spiritual world. For the nature spirits can be of great assistance to us in this goal, acting as 'emissaries of higher divine spiritual beings'.

ISBN 1-855840-18-9;   208pp;   £10.95